HOQP JUNKIE

Bob,

Thanks for buy
a copy of it.

HOOP

JUNKIE

The story of one man's career
working and having fun with
players, coaches and broadcasters
of the NBA

LEW SHUMAN

ISBN-13: 978-0692202845

ISBN-10: 0692202846

Library of Congress Control Number:

LCCN: 2014907151

Slidell, Louisiana

Published by Lewis A. Shuman

Cover Design by Leo Freeman

Dedication:

To my wife Sharyn for letting me play with the big boys all these years

Contents

Foreword

Hoop Junkie is about the NBA, its players, coaches, officials and broadcasters and was written by an individual who has spent most of his career working in sports television as a producer and director. Lew Shuman, aka The Cruise Director was my former Boston Celtics producer and director and he presents a humorous look behind the scenes as well as the occasional thought provoking... I didn't know that? You get to travel with players on their private charters, be with them as they win and lose both off and on the court and you get to sit in with members of the Basketball Hall of Fame. In addition you're taken to a world where no civilian has gone. What you will encounter is over 30 years of relationships and fond memories including: a legendary radio broadcaster who actually sets his pants on fire while on the air. Walk down Collins Avenue in Miami Beach with a player in scorching heat and stifling humidity wearing a mink coat just to be in vogue. As a reader you will sit in on a high-stakes card game where the pot is well over six figures. You will witness someone being ejected for throwing something at an official. And, you will get a sense of how the NBA operates along with who some of its characters are. This book is a fun read for both adults and students and will give you a different perspective on some of your own hoop heroes. The Author takes you back to witness his development in broadcasting and sports television producing and directing. Enjoy!

Bob Cousy
Worcester, Massachusetts

Acknowledgments

What most of you will read is based on first-hand experience. Some conversations, personal recollections and shared experiences were gathered while working with the people listed below: I am grateful for their assistance in helping me to loosen the cobwebs in my memory and providing aid and help filling in the blanks. For that assistance I'd like to acknowledge the following people who cooperated with me on this book: Randy Ayers, Barry Brodsky, Stephen Bulpett, Tom Carelli, Tommy Cooper, Bob Cousy, Mike Crispino, Scott Davis, Frank DiGraci, Mike Fine, Leo Freeman, Kenny Gattison, Mike Gminski, Bill Hurley, Eddie Johnson, David Jovanovic, Tim Kempton, Mike Kickirillo, Doug Lane, Steve Martin, Cedric Maxwell, Kevin McHale, Gil McGregor, Peter May, Joel Meyers, Shawn Oleksiak, Glenn Ordway, Drew Porche, Josh Richardson, Tod Rosensweig, Joe Quasarano, Sam Russo, Daniel Sallerson, Gil Santos, Howie Singer, Gerry Vaillancourt, Jan Volk, Terry Wiens , David Wesley.

Prologue

February, 16, 2014 was All Star Weekend for the NBA and the Basketball World had assembled in New Orleans for their annual star-studded celebration and extravaganza. The best of the best in basketball gathered to showcase their talents for the entire world to see. With an anticipated audience in over 200 countries and territories I was situated in one of fifteen mobile units located in the broadcast compound adjacent to the Smoothie King Center preparing to direct the television feed that would be carried by CCTV China.

My responsibility along with my assigned crew was to provide an estimated 50 million viewers in China with coverage of the 53rd NBA All Star Game. The announcers Weiping ZHANG and Zizhong HUANG along with my interpreters from NBA China Hongmei Shi and Cheng-yi "Gary" Yu went over what the folks at Beijing Control would expect from us. Once again I found myself in the director's chair only this time my talent for the broadcast would be speaking Mandarin. In addition to the game itself, Beijing asked that we emphasize showing the dancers, mascots and, when he came into the arena- Yao Ming. In the moments before we went on the air I sat back in my chair and paused to reflect over what I had accomplished in my long career.

My life was atypical of most people growing up. My days centered on my community and its people. Sports were a big part of my life. When the time came time to serve my country I, like thousands of other youth my age, willingly went off to serve. We did our duty honorably and we came home. Through it all, I knew what I wanted to do with my life and I persevered and eventually my dreams came true. I've been honored to work with some talented individuals in both broadcasting and sports.

As a group we laughed together and we wept for fallen comrades. I've travelled and worked with some of the greatest athlete's in the world. I was there when they shattered records and when they won and lost championships. I've witnessed first-hand the successful growth of the NBA. In fact when the first All Star Game was played in 1951 Bob Cousy was the highest paid player in the league earning around $75,000 between his regular salary and his endorsement from Randy Boat Shoes in Randolph, Massachusetts. Today, the highest paid player, Kobe Bryant earned an estimated $60 million dollars per year combined income from the Los Angeles Lakers and Nike. The business of basketball has been good for both the owners and the players.

It's hard to believe that from growing up in Boston I would be lucky to have succeeded in an industry that at times took its toll on individuals on a regular basis. I have 4 regional sports Emmys on my mantel and frankly, I must have done something right because I'm still here after forty-seven years working in the same profession.

So please, sit back and enjoy what The Grateful Dead album titled *"What a long strange trip it's been."* Allow me the poetic liberty to change it to say, "What a long WONDERFUL trip it's been."

Chapter 1

Dorchester Boy

Growing up in the Dorchester section of Boston was an experience shared by many, working-class children in cities all around the United States. Situated between Roxbury to the north and Mattapan to the south, The Blue Hill Avenue section of Dorchester was predominantly working class Jews.

Every corner from Franklin Field to Mattapan Square was a cultural oasis of Jewish ethnicity with its merchants pitching their wares. There was a mixture of English and Yiddish in the air. Shoppers at every corner were provided a savory, sensory delight as mothers with children in hand shopped the broad avenue of bakeries, delicatessens, fish mongers, and dairy stores along with dry goods outlets. All this secularism provided a cultural background for a youngster to grow and mature. For the average child, time was spent occupied in school both public and Hebrew.

There was little or no crime at all.

For the occasional mischievous youth who stepped out of line for some petty crime or misdemeanor and happened to be collard by Officer Riley; this was often followed by a trip to Boston Police Department's Station 19. This red brick fortress on Morton Street was a destination very few of us had ever seen.

Parents with children in trouble relied on visits to the Police Station by State Representative Julius Ansel or State Representative Samuel Harmon pleading on behalf of the misguided young man's family and eventually achieving the release of the delinquent. Upon release, most were met by a swift kick in the ass by an aggravated father.

In return, the parents were asked to vote on Election Day or better yet, help out the politician that arranged for the police to excuse the alleged perpetrator. All in all, the boys and girls of Dorchester grew up with a respect for the law.

We knew too just what our boundaries were.

Boston is a city of enclaves with various nationalities. Boston proper had its Brahmins' like the Lodges, Cabot's and the Saltonstalls. The North End and East Boston was Italian. South Boston was home for the Irish with the famed Bulger Family; William Bulger ran the State Senate while his brother James "Whitey" Bulger ran the Mob exempting no one from his torture, murder and extortion. Roxbury was the melting pot for the relatively small black community. Jamaica Plain, Hyde Park and Roslindale were the destinations for the upwardly mobile Irish who were nick-named the "Lace Curtain or Two-Toilet Irish" for their ability to prosper and move out of their inner-city domains.

West Roxbury and Brighton were considered the wealthier sections of Boston and were the destinations for many families who looked for better housing and schools.

While growing up in Dorchester our immediate concern was to the east. Just off Talbot Avenue were Codman Square, Ashmont Station and Fields Corner and to the West were Jamaica Plain and Roslindale two areas we often referred to as no man's land by my friends and me. But it was the east; that was an area to be avoided by the young protégés of Blue Hill Avenue as it was the edge of Irish Boston and its youth took great pride in whipping the little Jewish Boy's posteriors as they walked home from school.

Fighting back was easy. We had our own weapon. Education!

Education was the most important avenue for the entire Jewish Community. It was the way to progress upward and obtain success in a Yankee driven and Irish controlled hierarchy that was Boston. Boys attended the major high schools of the city; Boston English High School for the average student like me.

Boston Technical for the more science orientated and Boston Latin School for the gifted students. The Girls had their own Latin School as well as the Jeremiah Burke High School aka "The Jerri."

It was the goal of every family to insure that their children would receive a good solid education and that education would guarantee their upward mobility in Boston Society. We wanted to be the doctors, lawyers and educators; not the policeman, fireman or civil servants. That was our difference. It was not because we thought the jobs were below us; in Irish run Boston the doors were closed to most Jews wanting those public service jobs.

In addition to education, the other influential activity in our lives was sports. Sports played a critical part of our day-to-day existence. Whether it was listening to sports on radio or watching it on television as youngsters we were participating in organized sports.

There was Little League Baseball at Franklin Field, where on any given summer night numerous teams were formed from minor to major league. These teams ran onto the field with the names of our favorite clubs; Red Sox, Yankees and Cubs were stenciled on the heavy woolen uniforms and cherished by their young owners.

It was the badge of honor to bring that uniform home first as a point of pride that you made the team and secondly the dirtier the better to the dismay of all the mothers tasked with the job of laundering the uniforms. They had to be washed and ready for the next game.

Little League Baseball, basketball at the Hecht House and Pop Warner Football was the glue that held the youth of the community together. And, we had our sports heroes. While the Italians had boxer, Jake Lamota and the Irish pulled for John L. Sullivan, we looked up to our own for bragging rights.

Jewish athletes like Dodger Hall of Famer Sandy Koufax. Koufax was a Dodger for life. His entire career was spent between Brooklyn and Los Angeles.

His accolades included: (*Courtesy MLB-Baseball Reference.com)

Pitching for 11 Seasons,*

He was the first pitcher in the Major Leagues to pitch four no-hitters.*

He was a National League MVP in 1963.*

He won the Cy Young Award three times. This award Koufax earned was for all of Baseball not for either the National or American Leagues.*

More important to us, he was Jewish.

Sandy Koufax was a man who put his faith before his occupation. Faced with the dilemma of having to pitch or not to pitch in the World Series in 1965, Koufax decided he would not pitch in Game One because the game would be played on Yom Kippur, the most holy day in the Jewish calendar.

Yom Kippur was our Day of Atonement. Our day to ask for forgiveness and Koufax's decision was warmly supported in my community as well as, all Jewish Communities everywhere.

Another Athlete that the Jewish Community of Boston respected was one of their own: Simon "Si" Rosenthal. Rosenthal was Boston born and had a short-lived career as backup outfielder for the home town team, The Boston Red Sox. Si played only two seasons with the Red Sox. But it was not Si Rosenthal's baseball prowess that won over the community. It's what he did after baseball.

Si Rosenthal had a son Irwin Rosenthal. Irwin was a Marine stationed in the Pacific. He was just 19 years old when he was killed in 1943 in a South Pacific battle while fighting against the Japanese. While Si mourned, he decided he needed to do something for Irwin. At the age of 45, Si Rosenthal joined the Navy. As fate would have it, three months after the D-Day landings in 1944 while patrolling off the coast of Normandy the minesweeper Si was assigned to as an enlisted seaman ironically hit a floating mine. Si Rosenthal was severely wounded and left paralyzed for the rest of his life.

Si Rosenthal would end up spending his remaining days in a wheel chair devoting all his personal resources to help the poor and disadvantaged youth. I know first-hand of his charitable conscience and contributions. As a teen I was a willing participant in helping Si in his charitable work.

Si Rosenthal was living and breathing in our community and my friends and I had the pleasure of meeting this man and to appreciate the sacrifices he made. I was privileged to know Si Rosenthal.

As a teenager in 1964, I was a member of a boys club in Boston at the YMHA Hecht House that was named after him; The Si Rosenthal's. One of our charitable efforts was to help Si Rosenthal construct a gymnasium for underprivileged youth 1,500 miles away in tiny Bay St Louis, Mississippi. With our nickels and dimes from car washes, bake sales and raffles we contributed to assist Si's effort. Finally the gymnasium was completed and in return the Black Catholic Priests of Saint Augustine named the gymnasium in his honor.

Sadly as a footnote, in 1969 the Si Rosenthal Gymnasium was destroyed by the rampaging wind and water of Hurricane Camille. Gulf Coast communities like Pass Christian, Gulfport, Biloxi and Bay St Louis practically ceased to exist after the devastation that was Hurricane Camille. It was not until 2005 that these vulnerable communities again faced devastation this time from a wicked lady named Katrina. The irony is that fifty years later after our contributions were collected and sent to help build this gymnasium. I live a mere twenty minute drive from the site of where the Si Rosenthal Gymnasium once stood. Every time I drive by on Highway 90 East just below the Bay Bridge there on the right side heading into Pass Christian, Mississippi is where the gymnasium once stood, I still get a lump in my throat and a warm feeling when I think of what a group of Jewish teenagers from Boston did for a similar group of black children in Coastal Mississippi.

Sadly, Simon Rosenthal left this earth on April 7, 1969 at the young age of sixty-five while living at the Veterans Hospital in West Roxbury, Massachusetts. Boyhood friends relayed the information of his death and funeral to me while I was halfway around the world serving in the Army. With his passing, we remembered his love for the game and we followed his ardor and played baseball.

When we were not playing sports, we were thirsty for anything that brought our heroes to us. Scanning the daily newspapers like the Boston Globe, Boston Record-American and Boston Herald-Traveler we read the sports columns of writers Ray Fitzgerald, Tim Horgan, Sam Kane, Larry Claflin and Cliff Keane. Through these writers and many more like them we were transported to the games played and they satisfied our inquisitive thirst for sports knowledge.

Every day we poured over the sports columns and stories along with all the current statistics that our favorite players received for their exploits. We read about how Wilt Chamberlain scored 100 points over the New York Knicks at the Sports Arena in Hershey, Pennsylvania. Over the morning edition of the Boston Globe at our kitchen tables we held our breath with every at-bat by Roger Maris in 1961 as he chased Babe Ruth's record of sixty home runs in a season. There were columns about Wilma Rudolph tearing up the track in her quest for Olympic gold and we were there with Bill Mazeroski as his clutch home run finished off the dreaded Yankees in the World Series of 1960.

As television was just starting to come into its own, we relied heavily on the print media to provide us with our daily dose of sports information about our teams and individual player achievements.

We were thrilled whenever the opportunity came for us to meet and see our hero's close-up and live. Every year at the YMHA Hecht House on American Legion Highway in Dorchester there would be an annual Father and Son Breakfast and each year we'd be honored by the presence of members of one of our home teams. The gymnasium had been converted into a huge banquet hall with a raised head table for our guests and circular tables set up to accommodate ten people. Each table was set with paper plates and plastic cutlery. We were a working-class community and we could not afford the luxury of fine china and sterling silver. Coffee cups and juice glasses at the ready when we entered and took our seats first come-first served. I remember sitting with friends like Steve Feldman, Barry Brodsky, Phil Tatelman and our Fathers. This breakfast was an event for us. To borrow the cliché, we were dressed to the nines with jackets and ties. All of us hoping for the moment when we might be able to go up shake their hands and get the desired autograph we wanted. It was also an opportunity for us to spend precious time with our Dads.

This particular year 1960 our invited guests were the World Champion Boston Celtics. The Celtics were right in the middle of creating their dynasty of back-to-back championships and we were in awe. Imagine the thrill of rubbing elbows and breaking bread aka. Bagels and cream cheese with our heroes right before our eyes.

Wow! There was Bill Russell along with, Bob Cousy, the "Houdini of the Hardwood." Sitting next to him was Tommy Heinsohn and Jim Loscutoff.   Joining them, the master of it all; the coach complete with his famous Cigar, Arnold "Red" Auerbach. Basketball was an inner-city game and we were face-to-face with our heroes.

What did this story have to do with broadcasting and basketball? Well let's say a seed was planted.

Many evenings were spent by members of my generation lying in bed at night with their transistor radios and ear pieces listening to the game broadcasts from near and far with great announcers like Ken Coleman, Ernie Harwell, Jack Buck, Curt Gowdy and Marty Glickman.

For some of us it was the beginning of a love affair with an industry that would eventually provide a way to make a living doing what one loved-sports broadcasting.

After a mediocre academic career at Boston English High School, my high school guidance counselor and I concluded that college was not the answer. Was I a good student? No! To put it mildly, I wasn't the class clown but let's say I was not very disciplined with my studies. Math and I could not agree. No matter how hard I tried the end result was usually a failing mark. Even my girlfriend Carol Jaffe was sympathetic to my problem and she would spend hours tutoring me as I tried to understand all to no avail. Carol went on to become a teacher and I'm sure I was not the last student tutored by her during her four decade long career.

In High School, I gravitated toward sports. I tried out for the football team only to be told "thanks for trying out." I was too small and too slow. In the Spring I showed up for baseball tryouts to see if there was a place for me? Coach Bill Stuart of Boston English High asked me, "What is your position?"

I replied, "I can pitch!" Tossing me the ball, he said let's see what you've got?" I went out to the mound and proceeded to get pounded by the upper classman thus ending my short-lived baseball career.

Still, the desire to be involved in sports drove me. In my senior year, I was named Sports Editor of the English High Record; my job was to cover all the varsity sporting events and to write a review and report on them. I followed the "Blue and Blue" Basketball and Football squads and their schedules culminating with the football team's Thanksgiving Day Game against our arch rival Boston Latin School.

This Turkey Day tradition was the oldest and longest running high school football rivalry in the nation. Continuing my reporting duties, I was drawn to the basketball team both as a reporter and as the team's manager. Sitting at the end of the bench opened my eyes to another way to be a part of organized sports.

Was I street-smart with common sense? Yes! After school and on weekends I thought of myself as a hustler! I spent time shining shoes outside the famous G & G Delicatessen. The G & G was a gathering place for all the neighborhood politicians as well as national candidates at every major election. The G & G would be the last stop before the voters went to the polls. I have vivid memories of Presidential

Candidates Dwight Eisenhower, John Kennedy and Hubert Humphrey taking to the stage to deliver their message to the assembled voters.

I spent time on the street corners not hanging around but selling newspapers. Boston at the time was a four newspaper town. The Globe, Herald, Traveler and Record American were in fierce competition for readers. With morning and evening editions, there was an opportunity to make some money hustling papers for pennies in my pocket.

One date that I remember clearly is August 5, 1962. It was a typical hot and humid summer day in Boston. I was at my post at the corner of Morton Street and Blue Hill Avenue wrapping up my morning sales of the various Sunday Editions. Summer newspaper sales tended to be slow with people on vacation. This was not to be the case for this particular Sunday.

In the broadcast news world five bells on the AP or UPI wire machine usually meant something big had happened. In the newspaper business something big comes in the form of an extra edition. All of a sudden, the delivery trucks started to drop off bundles of Extras. The big news story; Marilyn Monroe was dead! Suddenly people wanted to buy the Extra editions to find out what little news there was of her death. For me it was the biggest day in my newspaper selling career. I was starting to get an itch!

Scratching

Did I have a goal? Yes! With all that was taking place in the news arena, I wanted to be a part of it. News events were splashed all over the front pages and on the television. We read and watched in amazement the Cuban Missile Crisis and the sinking of the Andrea Doria and it all gave me an idea. I was bitten by the broadcasting bug and I was determined to make a career out of it. I had to get close to broadcasting to learn. I was not interested in making money; at least not for the moment. I knew that by gravitating toward broadcasting television and radio stations, I would have an opportunity to see first-hand how they operated and secondly make acquaintances by being a pest.

Boston at the time was home for some of the best radio in the country. WMEX Color Radio with Arnie Ginsburg and a supporting crew that included: Melvin X Melvin, Larry Glick, Fenway and the man that invented talk radio-Jerry Williams. WMEX Radio and their competition down the dial at WBZ Radio were the main players in attracting young listeners. WBZ Radio with personalities Dave Maynard, Carl Desuze in the morning, and Dick Summer late into the night and the legendary Disc-Jockey, Bruce Bradley competed for our listening loyalty. We all remembered our summer adventures at Paragon Park at Nantasket Beach in Hull, Massachusetts. There was Bruce Bradley on remote with his faithful sidekick Rock Needleman playing the hit songs that we loved.

For me I wanted in, this was what I desired to do! This was the club I wanted to join.

Over at WMEX, Jerry Williams invited a live studio audience in as he broadcast his show from 10pm to 1am Monday through Fridays. I would be in that audience whenever I could.

During commercial breaks, Jerry would talk to the people in his audience. The audience was mostly regulars; me included would banter with Jerry discussing sports or the politics of the day. With his live studio guests of local politicians and phone calls from national known celebrities his listeners were treated to crazy telephone callers like Grace Queen of the Cockamamie's. His shows were serious and at times, light hearted. Jerry Williams owned the nighttime airways in Boston.

After a while Jerry took a liking to me and decided that I would be his Gopher. He gave me a nick-name calling me "Ants" because I couldn't sit still. He said I had "ants in my pants."

What does a Gopher do?

Simply put he *goes* for whatever the man wanted.

Coffee!

A pack of cigarettes!

A food order!

On some evenings I'd run down to Kenmore Square and pick up the early editions of Boston's then three newspapers.

One night, Jerry's Show was on remote. Originating from the Ballroom of the old Statler-Hilton Hotel in Park Square, it was an opportunity for the public to come out and meet and listen to Jerry live and in person. I was asked if I would be available to help out with the evening's festivities and of course I said yes. What they wanted me to do was babysit. Not in the conventional way but to meet an individual and make sure he was where he was supposed to be.

My assignment was to meet and greet a new up and coming Pop Singer by the name of Bobby Darin. Darin who was just starting his career was touring around the country promoting his hit song-Mack the Knife. More than that; to a whole generation he was married to teen heart-throb Sandra Dee. Standing outside the hotel's main entrance waiting for his car to arrive I was really nervous. I had never met a real-live recording artist in the flesh. After a short while waiting a plain old Impala sedan pulled up and out from the passenger seat popped Bobby Darin.

I greeted him "Hello Mister Darin!"

He responded "Hi, who are you?"

I added, "I'm Lew and I'm here to meet you and take you into where the show is being broadcast from."

"Let's Go!" He said!

We proceeded into the hotel and made our way to the holding room that had been set aside for his use. We continued some small talk about Boston, the Red Sox and he indicated he was from Philadelphia and loved his Philadelphia teams too. I took his coat and scarf placed it carefully on a chair as we both sat down and waited for the word to bring Bobby into the ballroom. It was time! We walked out of the holding room and into the ballroom and the audience went wild as he was introduced to the admiring crowd. Jerry's interview went smoothly and in an instant, we were back in the holding room where I assisted him into his coat and scarf. We walked together out to his waiting car and he turned, shook my hand and thanked me for being a good host.

What I recall the most about that evening; he remembered my name and his scarf. The scarf was the softest material I had ever touched. I guessed later it was most likely cashmere. Unfortunately, Bobby Darin died at the early age of thirty-seven due to failing health caused by an earlier childhood bout with rheumatic fever. On a side note, Sandra Dee never remarried after her love Bobby Darin passed away.

I relished hanging with Jerry Williams at his WMEX radio studio as his Gopher.

WMEX was located on Brookline Avenue in the same building as Fenway Park. While there I had the opportunity to sit in, watch, listen and learn. My twice-nightly runs to the White Castle where the wait-staff knew exactly what I wanted when I walked in; 1 large extra light coffee-no sugar just the way Jerry liked it. Most nights before Jerry's 10pm show I'd try to get to the studio early where I'd spend part of my evenings sitting in with the number one radio personality in Boston, Arnie "Woo Woo" Ginsburg.

During commercials we would trade jokes and share one-liners. It was amazing the size of the audience that was out there listening to Arnie's "Night Train" Show and they were all eating hamburgers bought from his faithful sponsor, Adventure Car Hop in Saugus while snuggling with their favorite person at the submarine races all over greater Boston.

I was stung! I wanted to be a broadcaster.

Right after graduating from high school I signed up to attend Northeast Broadcasting School. Northeast was owned and operated by veteran Boston newscaster Victor Best and his able-bodied manager Vincent Rafferty. Northeast Broadcasting was your typical fast-track eight month long "trade school" that prepared people rather quickly. It was for folks who did not have the time or the money to devote to a four year program at a college or university. And, I was in a hurry to get into the business. I was nick-named Super Jew by Vince for my aggressive ability to take on any task thrown my way. With that aggressiveness I was the first in my class from Northeast Broadcasting School to land a real job in broadcasting.

WKBG-TV Channel 56 was a start-up UHF station in Boston that was a joint venture between Kaiser Industries and the Boston Globe Newspaper Company.

I showed up for my interview at the Channel 56 Studios which were located on the second floor at 1050 Commonwealth Avenue in what was once a dress and apparel manufacturing plant. Sitting there in my ill-fitting suit I nervously interviewed with the Station's Chief Engineer, Max Thomas. After the usual small talk on why I wanted the job, Max said he was going to give me a chance.

I was to be a Stage Manager for WKBG-TV Channel 56. It was an entry-level position that included: cueing talent, setting up sets and yes, I even followed the animal acts cleaning up after they did their business on the studio floor.

The station signed on the air December 21, 1966 and my career was off and running. Learning audio, video, camera and video tape all the while I was working in live television and loving every minute of it.

It was also the time I had the opportunity to work with and meet a true broadcast legend: Jack Parr. It was 1968 and Eugene McCarthy was running for President of the United States. His campaign office had made arrangements for McCarthy to rent our studio to record his fifteen minute announcement describing his political aspirations. As part of his announcement McCarthy would be introduced by Jack Parr. With everything in place, Parr entered the studio, casually greeted everyone and sat down to introduce Eugene McCarthy.

I took my position next to the lead camera slapped on my headsets and waited for my instructions from the director in the control room.

"Stand by!" I repeated the instruction loudly for all to hear including Jack Parr.

I begin the countdown, "Five, Four Three, Two, One. Cue Talent!" and I pointed my finger at Jack to begin.

Jack Parr began, "Good Evening Everyone, I'd like to introduce you to my good friend Eugene McCarthy." Just then, we all heard this metal-to-metal scratching noise that interrupted Jack to where he said "What the hell was that?" We immediately stop the recording and it was up to me to explain what happened. Remember our studios were located above an old dress and apparel factory. Well the first floor was still operating and on occasion we would hear those rolling racks of clothing and the noise made it upstairs to our studio. Parr shook his head and smiled and said, "Upstaged by a dress" we waited for the noise to cease and proceeded to finish the videotaping without another incident.

Throughout all these experiences I was a sponge!

I tried to absorb everything. I also decided that I wanted to be in television rather than radio. Just then my fledgling broadcast career came to a complete stop.

Chapter 2

The Launch

Hut two, three, four

In the short term external pressures were pressing me and my peers in other directions. In 1968, the United States was deeply involved in Southeast Asia and Vietnam.

I was past eighteen years old, physically fit and very draft eligible. The Selective Service Law required us to register at age 18. My status was 1A. Well, my number came up and I was notified of my potential induction into the armed forces. Frankly, I was scared of the Draft and the chance that I would be sent to Vietnam as an infantry soldier or as they were called an "11 Bravo Grunt."

I wanted to be in control of my own destiny.

Not wanting to wander too far from my love of broadcasting, the patriotic side of me arranged for a visit to my nearest Army Recruiting Office hoping to continue in a similar field of endeavor. After several negotiations on my future army career path, I selected Motion Picture Equipment Repair as my future military occupation. After Basic Training I was guaranteed the school of my choice and the occupation requested. On June 23, 1968 at the Boston Army Base on Summer Street I and quite a few others stood in front of a Marine Corps Major held up our right hands and "swore to support and defend the Constitution of the United States... so help me God." I enlisted! Welcome to the United States Army Private E-1 Lewis A. Shuman RA (Regular Army) 11625972.

After eight grueling weeks in the hot, unforgiving humid air of Fort Knox, Kentucky I successfully completed my Basic Training. I moved on to my next stop Fort Monmouth, New Jersey for my Advanced Individual Signal Corp Training. After completing eight weeks at Fort Monmouth, New Jersey I was ready for my next assignment. Fully expecting to be deployed to Vietnam, I was surprised when my orders came down that I would be assigned to The 48th Tactical Command located in the Southern German Town of Schwabisch Gmund. My Unit would be located adjacent to the Communist Czechoslovakian border and our mission was to safeguard Western Europe from the potential threat from the Soviet Union. One week before I was to ship out, my orders for Germany were "flagged" and rescinded. I was given new orders to report to the Transportation Office at Fort Monmouth to prepare for overseas processing for new duty station-Tehran, Iran.

Iran?

I never heard of it nor did I know where it was? After looking it up on a map at the Base Library, I began an odyssey that would change me and my life.

The assignment was not what I had expected. I was informed I had been promoted to Specialist (E-4) and would be travelling in uniform with a Diplomatic Passport and would be flying not on a MAC (Military Airlift Command) troop flight but on a commercial Pan American Jet Clipper. I was given tickets and instructed to make my way to John F. Kennedy Airport and board Flight Number 114 out of JFK. I departed New York on January 28, 1969 at 1830 hours (6:30pm) with stops in Paris, Rome, and Ankara and eventually 26 hours later I landed in Tehran, Iran on January 29, 1969. I was greeted at the airport by the soldier I would be replacing-Ricardo Childress. His tour of duty was up and he was heading back to the States.

I was assigned to the ARMISH/MAAG Support Service Division Signal Office. The Signal Office's job was to provide radio, telephone and motion picture support to all the MAAG units in Tehran, Field Teams and our Embassy.

In the history of the Army, there have only been seven MAAG's. They were MAAG Laos, MAAG China, MAAG Cambodia, MAAG Vietnam, MAAG Indochina, MAAG Thailand and MAAG Iran. These exclusive and elite Military Advisory Assistance Groups were put in place to advise and support the host country's military. MAAG Iran was no different. We were there to support the Shah of Iran and his military machine. With Field Team's at all major bases in Iran, the American presence was everywhere. Teams in Shiraz, Esfahan, Tabriz, Abadan and other locales were liaisons to their Iranian counterparts either at their army bases, ports or their airfields.

MAAG Iran was headed by an Army Major General, Hamilton Twitchell. Under Twitchell's command were two Brigadier Generals the legendary Theodore Mataxis who was with the Americal Division in Vietnam and Air Force Brigadier Roy N. Casbeer and Navy Captain, R. S. Harward. All were there to administer each branch's training and support efforts. The command structure was heavy with Senior Grade Officers and Senior NCO's (Non Commissioned Officers). It was a rarity to see any Junior Grade Officers or low-ranking enlisted personnel. All personnel assigned were specialists in their MOS's (Military Occupation Specialty) and specifically selected for this assignment after security clearances were issued.

Field team duty was considered a hardship tour without dependents. For those stationed in Tehran it was considered a safe duty station and most married members of the MAAG were accompanied by their dependents. Nearly all of the military dependants of school age attended the Tehran American School. We had our own hospital and commissary. Our social lives centered on either The PKEOM (Persian Knights Enlisted Open Mess) and the American Officers Club; both were our oasis in Tehran for socializing and dining. We were free to wander and explore the city and its sites.

Enlisted personnel and officers accompanied by dependents lived in their own rented homes or apartments in communities in North Tehran like Darroous, Davoodiyeh and Vanak. For the single un-accompanied NCO's we lived in a team house in the Zarrin Neighborhood. There were no barracks. Our spacious team house came with a swimming pool, maid service, drivers and dining facilities. We were living on the local economy. And, we were living well. The Team House was in a neighborhood of Americans and middle-class Iranian families and we shopped together at the same stores. We socialized with our American friends and we took the time to try and meet our Iranian neighbors. There was a genuine admiration of Americans by the Iranian people.

I'll never forget one night in June of 1969. I had spent the evening at the home of my girlfriend Kathy MacDonald having dinner with her father, Bill a career Air Force Sergeant, her mother Mary and younger brother Larry. She lived in the Davoodiyeh neighborhood and it was about a two mile hike down Shemiran Avenue back to the Team House. On most night's I'd make the walk back to the Team House but once in a while I would flag down an orange Peykan Taxi and jump in.

The driver would greet me with the usual "*Salam!*" Hello!

I responded with "*Motshekerum, Hal e Shoma*!" Thank you and how are you?"

Then I told him in my best Farsi "*Aga, Zarrin Club, Koochie Zarrin, Zootbash!*' which translated to Mister take me to the Zarrin Club (our neighborhood) on Zarrin Street quickly.

On this special night of July 20, 1969 I was very proud to be an American. The trio of Neil Armstrong, Buzz Aldrin and Michael Collins had just landed on the Moon and I felt connected to them. Looking up at the big full moon the driver sensed what I was looking at and interrupted the quiet to say,: "*Amerikia, Kheili Khoob*" (America is very good) at the same time pointing his finger up at the Moon and smiling. The Iranian people that I met were genuine and kind and they loved talking to us even if we had difficulty with Farsi, we all made an effort to communicate.

As far as my broadcast career, well things always do fall into place. While I was officially attached to the Signal Office under the command of Captain John Mackey and Sergeant First Class Harold Copeland in addition to my assigned duties as a Motion Picture Repair Technician, I was given the opportunity to be the host of a nightly Radio program on the AFRTS (American Forces Radio and Television Service). I was the voice behind the radio programs Upbeat '69 and Scene '70 spinning the latest Department of Defense authorized Rock and Roll music on AFRTS AM 1555. I was on-the-air evenings 7-8pm and loving it. My audience was the large Military and American Community in Iran as well as the general Iranian population that included a steady stream of telephone calls from young and beautiful raven haired Iranian women who were eager to practice their English and possibly the opportunity to meet an American GI.

I spent just over eighteen months in a country that I learned to love. From the Caspian Sea in the North to the shores of the Shatt al Arab River on the Persian Gulf I found the Iranian people to be warm, outgoing and friendly. When it came time to leave Iran, there were ten fingers holding onto the runway at Mehrabad Airport the day of my departure. It broke my heart to see the turmoil that evolved after our Embassy takeover and the Iranian Revolution that followed.

I finished my military service at Fort Ord in beautiful Monterey, California. I was attached to the Army Experimentation Command and our job was to provide motion picture documentation on weapons being tested. After a brief eight months at Fort Ord I was discharged honorably and I returned to Boston to continue my broadcast career.

Ready One, Take One

It was there back at Channel 56 where my hoop dreams started to come true.

They say opportunity only knocks once and that was the case for me. After being discharged from the army and returning to WKBG-TV in Boston my career started to flourish. With my steady job came marriage and personal stability. I was working on the technical side doing several jobs that included: technical director, audio and video tape along with numerous live remote assignments. Even though I was working hard, I was not happy. Sitting next to the directors that were assigned to do our live programming I began to see and feel that I could do their job and probably do it better. I was cocky! Just my luck, a staff director position became available and I jumped at the chance to move up. Our Production Manager at the time Joe Quasarano had the confidence in me to give me my shot at directing. I did not waste the opportunity.

As time passed, my confidence level and ability grew with every show I directed. It was a tremendous learning environment. One day I would be doing a live remote from an automobile dealership or a live "Kiddie" show in the studio and the next day I'd be at Conti Forum on the campus of Boston College working a Big East Basketball Game. We would also find ourselves at the Boston Arena for a WHA, World Hockey Association Boston Whalers Hockey Game. With all this, my plate was full. Timing was everything and that was the case with local sports contracts in Boston.

The Boston Celtics Television Rights on WBZ-TV had expired and were to be opened up for bidding. WKBG had ceased to exist as new owners and new call letters greeted the viewers of Boston. WKBG TV became WLVI-TV and was now the station of record. Its new owners were the Gannett Publishing Company. Gannett was interested in moving the station in another direction and that included sports broadcasting.

At the time, WLVI TV's General Manager was a tough, street-wise little Irishman named Gerry Walsh. Walsh had a vision for the station and the chutzpah to aggressively go after the Celtics television rights.

Walking into Red Auerbach's Office in the old Boston Garden on Causeway Street, Walsh played his cards perfectly. Red liked what he saw in front of him especially the zeros and commas on the Rights check that was sitting on his desk. Walsh's persistence paid off and culminated in the signing of a five year deal for Channel 56 to televise all the Celtics road games commencing with the 1985-1986 Season. The Celtics were hot! Coming off of another World Championship in 1984, the timing couldn't have been better. Channel 56 would be the recipient of thousands of advertising dollars that the team would generate and bring into the station's coffers. It was not un-common for an advertiser to pay a spot rate of $3,000.00 plus for a thirty second unit for his advertisement in the games. That $3,000.00 figure was un-heard of at the time especially for a UHF station whose other programming consisted mainly of old movies, some sports and re-runs of network syndications. Needless to say this period was a very lucrative time for WLVI-TV.

So where did I fit in to this equation?

As a kid, I had the opportunity to play basketball on the same hardwood court that was home to the Celtics. Our opponents were from the neighborhoods of Boston and included: The Charlestown Boys' and Girls' Club and the Chinatown YMCA. "Red" Auerbach and the Celtics were gracious enough to allow us to play after school and we would receive free balcony tickets to that night's game. There were no locker room or showers for us and we changed in the stands from our street clothes to our uniforms. After our game we would dash across Causeway Street to Joe and Nemo's for a steamed hot dog and burger after which we joined the rest of the "gallery gods" in the balcony at the Garden to cheer for our guys in green. After the game, we would all hop on the "T" at North Station for the subway ride home to Dorchester.

Now, for once my being in the right place at the right time paid off. There was no one on staff at Channel 56 who had the desire or ability to take over the task of producing and directing live sports. Seeing the opportunity I jumped in, requested and was given the responsibility of producing and directing the World Champion Boston Celtics.

With this awesome responsibility came the "perks" of the job; getting to travel with a professional sports team, staying at first-class hotels and eating at the best restaurants all over the United States. I would have the opportunity to work with some very talented individuals.

Play by Play Announcers like Gil Santos who just retired after 36 years as the radio voice of the New England Patriots, Mike Crispino, Greg Gumbel, Andy Musser, Tom Mees, Neil Funk, Marc Zumoff, Steve Martin, Bob Licht and Joel Meyers would be my teachers throughout my broadcast career contributing to my continuous learning curve.

Then there were my distinguished Analysts: first and foremost, Bob Cousy. "The Cooz," really helped in my understanding of the game of basketball. Jack Ramsay, Steve Mix, Gil McGregor, Mike Gminski and Gerry Vaillancourt all contributed to me being better at my job.

So, you're probably wondering where all this was leading to? I have been both graced and gifted. When was the last time you met someone who at the age of 13 new what they wanted to do in life?

I have over 30 years experience working for three NBA teams; The Boston Celtics, The Philadelphia 76ers and The Charlotte/New Orleans Hornets/Pelicans. I have over 2,500 professional basketball games on my resume as a producer, director or administrator. I've come to know players and coaches both active and retired from all the teams in the NBA. In my tenure in sports broadcasting, I've experienced first-hand some unique and entertaining individuals. With all the travel and time spent together there were some great stories that occurred and I've accumulated many of them over my career. I've kept notes and what you will read will be first-hand recollections with the mentioned individuals as well as, people who shared stories with me during my career.

If you're looking for a salacious tell-all type of book, this is not it. If you're interested in a few "chuckles and grins," along with the occasional I didn't know that! Then enough about me, let's begin.

Chapter 3

Oh, Johnny!

Johnny Most

Of all the Talent that I worked with the one that stands out among all the others: the irascible, legendary Johnny Most. Johnny's roots were New York City and Dewitt Clinton High School. Like most young men of his generation he volunteered and served in the Army Air Corps. Johnny was a decorated veteran of aerial combat as a gunner on a B-24 Liberator over Europe in World War II.

A protégé of the late, Marty Glickman, Johnny was most noted for his grainy voice that always started his basketball broadcasts with his classic sign on "Hi there once again, this is Johnny Most high above courtside…where the Boston Celtics are getting set to do basketball battle." Johnny was the ultimate homer.

To him basketball broadcasting was an epic battle of the forces of good over evil. The good guys always wore green (Celtics) and the evil happened to be the particular opponent of the moment. For Johnny, every opponent and its players were the bad guys and Johnny let you know that. No one was protected from the tongue lashings the Johnny spewed at the enemy of his beloved Boston Celtics.

At playoff time, he referred to Ervin "Magic" Johnson of the hated Lakers as "Crybaby" Johnson.

 Whenever the Celtics played the Washington Bullets, his two favorite targets were Jeff Ruland and Rick Mahorn who he called "McFilthy and McNasty."

His displeasure with the players on the Detroit Pistons was also evident.

Noted for their aggressive, physical play, Johnny would lash out in his raspy voice to call Bill Lambier a "dirty rotten player" and more so his pure disdain for Isaiah Thomas whom he constantly referred to as "Little Lord Fauntleroy."

For those of us who knew him he was a character of the old school of broadcasting.

On the road, Johnny rated the team hotel as five star if they had a 24 hour coffee shop. Since most of us in the business were nocturnal by our schedules, it was a common site to find Johnny with his ever present cup of coffee and cigarette sitting in booth and holding a conversation with a total stranger.

As Johnny grew older his irascible persona changed as well. Traveling as a group we all looked out for each other; including Johnny. We kidded him a lot but we all watched out for him too.

Here are few stories that we can tell about Johnny with a smile.

In 1988, the Celtics were in Madrid Spain to play in the League's first-ever international exposure; The McDonalds Open. Our opponents would be Spain's Real Madrid and the Yugoslavian National Team whose roster included players Vlade Divac, Drazen Petrovic and Tony Kukoc. It would be one of the earliest introductions of European players to the competition of the NBA. We were eager to broadcast back to Boston on both television and radio.

The NBA Public Relations people set up a meeting for all the broadcasters to become acquainted with the Spaniards and the

Yugoslavs. And, at this meeting, we would learn the correct phonetic pronunciation of the players. A meeting Johnny decided to skip.

Well folks, Johnny was old school alright. His idea of game preparation was to walk into the gym, game notes rolled up under his arm, take his seat at the broadcast position and go on the air. To this day, his radio "call" in Madrid remains as one of the classic radio miss-performances ever.

With his partner Analyst Glenn Ordway and Producer Tom Carelli sitting next to him, Johnny began his game description and together their jaws dropped. Here is what listeners back in Boston were treated to:

"Hi everyone, this is Johnny Most high above courtside in Madrid, Spain..."

Continuing his play by play presentation it sounded like this. "Now, quickly out in the middle it goes to ahhh, (pause) the little guard ahhhh, Uperdovich (sic). Now quickly to the big guy and now to a lefty and he lost the ball...but it's picked up by the little fellow."

Without missing a beat, Johnny deadpans into the microphone, "Oh boy! I'm having trouble with these names." I guess Johnny should've gone to the meeting. His partner, Glenn Ordway did his best to help out and salvage the broadcast but by then it was too late.

Johnny's love affair with tobacco leads to one of the more humorous moments in his broadcast career. Johnny was a heavy smoker. Before arenas around the League put a stop to smoking it was very common for people to light cigarettes, cigars and pipes up at a game and, that was no different for Johnny. I'm sure some people can remember the days when a dull blue haze hung over an arena's playing court as most people attending games were smokers. It became a regular joke to pick on Johnny because of his smoking.

At airports, we'd wait for him to go into the Men's Room to sneak a smoke then one of us, usually Gil Santos our television play-by-play man would walk in, bang on the stall door and yell, "it's the police are you smoking in there? And Johnny as repentant as a schoolboy would say "No Officer," as you heard the flushing of the toilet. We would give him gentle ribbing when we could on the subject of smoking.

One night in Dallas, Texas at the old Reunion Arena, the laws with regards to smoking in public places had just been changed to make it illegal to light up in a public place. Not that Johnny would pay attention to any new laws concerning smoking in public places. He would always light up and hold his cigarette under his broadcast table and when he could, he'd take a drag and down under the table the cigarette would go again.

Well, on this particular night, coming out of a commercial break, Johnny was nowhere to be found. He had sneaked out to grab a quick puff. Analyst Glenn Ordway told Studio Producer Tom Carelli that Johnny was not at the broadcast table. Where is he cries Carelli over the talk-back system? Glenn was forced to take over and started describing the play-by-play action in Johnny's absence. With the game back under way, out of the corner of his eye Ordway noticed Johnny being escorted back to his seat by two rather large and burly Texas State Troopers. He sits down slaps on his microphone on and mind you, Johnny is on the air live!

Without missing a beat in between plays Johnny begins to wail "there were four hundred and ninety-five robberies and two hundred and fifty rapes being committed in the State of Texas today and all they have to do is stop me from smoking." Johnny rants on just how his rights were being violated by the folks in Texas who would not let him smoke. Continuing, Johnny was claiming a Communist Conspiracy to take away his right to smoke. Venting on-the-air how un-American it was to demand that he stop smoking.

I don't want to say we picked on Johnny but let's just say when it came to his smoking we occasionally exhibited childish behavior. Danny Ainge was constantly telling Johnny that tobacco was no good and eventually it would kill him. It went in one ear and out the other as far as Johnny was concerned. Danny the prankster decided to do something to pester Johnny for smoking. We were on a flight to a game when Ainge decided to set up his prank. With smoking banned on all commercial flights Johnny would always have an unlighted cigarette dangling between his two fingers. His standard response to the flight attendant who glanced toward him and his cigarette was "relax, it ain't lit babe."

As the flight progressed and with Johnny sound asleep Danny gently sneaked up to him and retrieved Johnny's pack of cigarettes from his shirt pocket. He then took out a cigarette and proceeded to insert a couple of "loads." He replaced the cigarette in such a way as it would be the next one Johnny would retrieve and gingerly returned the pack to his shirt pocket. Meanwhile, our flight lands and we all head for the bus that's outside the terminal. Johnny is outside at the curb enjoying his first cigarette the one that was dangling in his hand on the plane. He finishes that cigarette and pulls out another from his pack. We are all glued to the windows of the bus like children staring into a candy store waiting for something to happen. Johnny lights up the cigarette, take a deep drag and…nothing. As he drops his hand down to his side-BANG! The loads explode. Johnny, who was having hearing problems at the time, looked incredulously at the remainder of what had been a cigarette and uttered an expletive. He chucked the remnants to the curb and causally lit another as if nothing had happened.

Well, it was his smoking that led up to one of funniest incidents ever on live radio.

At the time, Johnny and his partner Glenn Ordway along with their Engineer, Doug Lane were sitting "High above Courtside" in the old Boston Garden when unbeknown to Johnny, during one of his verbal tirades, he dropped a lit cigarette in his lap and smoke started to swirl as his polyester pants caught on fire. On-the-air we were treated to the first-time ever of a play-by-play man's pants catching on fire and his description of the action. Surrounded by smoke and fire Glenn Ordway is hysterical in trying to inform the listeners of what was happening to Johnny all the while a basketball game was in progress. Not having learned from his experience, Johnny did the very same thing the next evening. Two games in a row Johnny had set his polyester pants on fire while on-the-air. It was a sight to see at the very next game, Ordway and Lane are sitting courtside next to Johnny with red fire hats on their heads in a mock tribute to Johnny.

This Johnny Most story supports my theory that some people are made of steel; so to was Johnny Most.

Starting the 1985 Season, Johnny was becoming increasingly hard of hearing especially on his left side. It was becoming obvious something was definitely wrong with Johnny and it centered on his hearing. Whenever we would get into a conversation with him it always turned into a

"Huh? Huh?" "What! What?"

Or, he would ask us, "come around this side so I can hear you better."

We were all at a loss as to what his problem was?

In Broadcasting one of the most valuable tools for the broadcaster is what is called an IFB. Its proper name is Interruptible Fold Back. Basically it allows the talent to hear instructions from his studio on content, cueing (when to start talking) as well as, listening to the production crew or producer. This is accomplished a couple of different ways.

On most televised sporting events, the viewer usually sees the talent wearing headset microphones. These microphones provide the talent with the ability to hear themselves and their partner while screening out crowd noise and superfluous clamor. Additionally, the IFB is connected to the headsets for instruction. In the world of news and live shots aka ENG (Electronic News Gathering) talent traditionally wears a smaller, belt-attached ear device. This device consists of a wire connected to a listening tube of clear, thin plastic tubing that connects to an ear bud or detachable nipple as it is referred to and inserted in the reporter's ear and serves the same way as a headset microphone would too. You've seen these devices on reporters, anchors and weather forecasters in their studios' and out in the field. It's that little curly-cue of clear plastic that you see attached to their shirt or dress and into their ear.

Back to Johnny!

More and more frustrated at his hearing loss, Johnny finally decided to visit the Celtics Team Doctor, Tom Silva. Now, this hearing problem has been going on for months and Johnny's frustration was visible. After a very short examination by the doctor the mystery of Johnny's loss of hearing in his left ear was solved. With a little prodding and pulling, the Doctor successfully removed an embedded ear bud nipple from his Ear. It seems that Johnny had inserted it in his ear for some live shot a few months back and it had lodged itself in his ear. After the nipple's removal from his ear canal, he was asked how his hearing was. Johnny replied. "It's a miracle, I can hear again." Johnny had been living with this little plastic implement in his ear canal for months.

My final Johnny Most story is a doozy.

Toward the end of his illustrious broadcast career, the years of no sleep, cigarettes, bad diet and yes, the occasional cocktail had taken its toll on Johnny Most resulting in his suffering a stroke. The Stroke did not deter Johnny from continuing to do his job as the Celtics' Play-by-Play voice. Though Johnny was physically limited by the stroke; Johnny performed the best he could with the physical limitations that he had. He could walk, talk and drive all with the use of only one good arm.

Here's where it became very interesting.

After a long West Coast road trip, we're set to open a home stand at Boston Garden when Johnny walks into the Press Room, his arm bandaged, his face bruised and battered. We asked him what had happened. It seems that Johnny on his drive home from the airport had an automobile accident on an icy road and he slid off into a ditch. Concerned, we asked Johnny what happened and how he ended up in a wreck? Johnny proceeded to tell us, "It all happened in a flash... a) I was trying to shift gears while b) smoking a cigarette, and c) holding a cup of coffee while driving a standard transmission-all with one arm."

The media folks listening in the Press Room burst into laughter as did Johnny realizing just how funny it sounded.

Chapter 4

Games, Fashion and Whatever

Scrabble

Players were not immune to faux pas while travelling. With their competitive spirit, it was a common sight to see groups of players casually playing cards and other interesting games. The players loved to play the games of Tonk and BooRay. Tonk is a form of Rummy. To win, the player needs to have the fewest points with the cards being worth face value. In BooRay, you win tricks and books after anteing.

Players were always looking for new ways to fill time on long airplane rides besides playing cards. Some fellows started bringing on Scrabble Boards. Not the ones that you have in your home closets but a smaller scale magnetic version that was easier to play with and not subject to pieces flying all over the place after being bumped or worse; air turbulence.

Travel back in the old days of the NBA was by commercial airlines. There were no charters like the players enjoy today. We travelled as a group and the Head Trainer was in charge of travel. He would hand out the tickets and boarding passes. Whenever possible everyone would receive a coveted aisle seat. Seniority dictated seating. Veteran players and the Head Coach were granted the most desired First-Class Cabin with the extra legroom that it provided.

On this particular Celtics flight, Ray Williams, a twelve year veteran of the NBA was signed by Boston after a trade. He decided to challenge his teammates to a game of Scrabble. We're on a Boston to Los Angeles flight and Ray with his magnetic board in hand proceeded to organize a game with a few of his teammates.

Well, you can imagine the competition was intense. Players were doing their best to maximize their points in hopes of winning. Suddenly the cabin erupts in laughter. We can't imagine what could be so funny during a game of scrabble? As the laughter continues, one player in a tutorial tone said, "Ray, there is no such word as "*Cap'n Crunch.*"

Continuing the game as it moved from one player to another it came back around to Ray who placed the word "axes" on the board.

Immediately Kevin McHale skeptically asked, "*Axes*? What kind of a word is *axes*?" Ray responded, "You know *axes*."

McHale then asked Ray, "Use it in a sentence." Ray's retort was classic, "You got to pay your *axes*." End of game!

Anthony Mason

NBA players have style. Just ask them? Almost all have their own tailors that keep them supplied with dress wear and casual clothing. Most players when dressed up could make the cover of GQ (Gentlemen's Quarterly). Then, there are the players who go one step beyond their peers. Their dress is an indication of status. The have some very serious disposable income to spend on designer threads that they wear solely so they'll be noticed.

Anthony Mason played for 13 seasons and I had the pleasure of knowing Anthony when he was with the Hornets for four seasons from 1996-2000. He was a fierce competitor and tenacious rebounder. He reached all-star status once in his career and he was a contradiction in many ways; especially in his dress.

On one trip to Miami to play the Heat right after the All-Star break, most of the players and coaches were travelling from Charlotte on the team's charter. Others returned from the All Star break reappearing on their own. It was there in Miami on South Beach where we witnessed just what it meant to be decadent in your dress attire.

Arriving at the Miami FBO Millionaire Air we deplaned and boarded our busses that would transport us to the team hotel. NBA teams and most other professional organizations utilize charter busses to transport the entire travelling party rather than relying on each individual to provide their own transportation to their destination.

There were the usual two buses waiting. One bus was exclusively for the players and coaches and a second bus was for us media types, staff and invited guests. We were on the second bus as Team Equipment Manager David "Big Shot" Jovanovic and Team Trainer Terry Kofler loaded the busses with all the travelling party's luggage and team gear. Once everything was loaded we were on our way.

Our destination was South Beach where we were all looking forward to a little warmth and a nice dinner. After leaving chilly, damp Charlotte we anticipated being in the 80 plus degree heat and the never ending South Beach Nightlife.

On the ride to the hotel most folks occupied their time by reading or listening to music on their headsets. Other chatted casually about everything from the weather to the game that was to be played the following evening or where they would be going that evening.

As I had mentioned, not all players were on the flight because of the All-Star break. With our bus slowly moving down Collins Avenue in Miami Beach all of a sudden out of the bus window someone noticed Anthony Mason and gives everybody a heads up. Sure enough, there was Anthony with his posse strolling down Collins Avenue toward our hotel in the 80 degree heat and humidity wearing a stunning black mink jacket with the number 14 stenciled on his back.

This was a prime example of style dictating over need. When we were closer, we could see the sweat rolling of Anthony but he didn't care. He was in style and that's all that mattered. We later found out that in addition to the black mink, he also owned a similar silver mink jacket with the inscription "Mace" on the back.

BooRay

Players love to play cards and one card game they really enjoy is BooRay. In its simplest form BooRay is a game where the participants ante and deal, have the option to draw or pass eventually deciding whether to play. The ultimate goal is to win tricks or books with the highest card and not be trumped. As a player you have the option of getting out before drawing your cards. If no one wins a hand the game progresses and the pot continues to grow in value.

Players love the challenge and the competition and are not afraid to put down a little of their per diem money to cover a bet in a friendly card game. Today's NBA player receives $129.00 per day while traveling. This is their mad money!

In a story related to me by one of my Television Analysts David Wesley. David was a fourteen plus year veteran and had played for five NBA teams including: New Jersey, Boston, Charlotte/New Orleans, Houston and Cleveland. A get-in-your-face defender David also was a double-digit scoring threat his entire career. David too was a bone fide BooRay player and as he explained it:

"We were on a short, one-hour flight to Memphis…" The card players with me were: Baron Davis, Steven Smith, Darrell Armstrong and Rookie Shammon Williams." Let the BooRay begin!

"We're playing for short money… Ante is just $5.00 per person per hand."

Everyone involved is having a good time when Steve Smith pipes in,

"You're all chicken, let's change the rules, too many of you are getting out so from now on, everyone stays in and we're raising the Ante to $20.00."

As David continued, "So now, every pot is in the $80.00 to $100.00 range."

Remember, there were five players contributing to this pot.

David emphasized, "It (the pot) ended up getting big, REALLY BIG!"

"The first time I got caught it was 15 not 15 dollars but $15,000.00."

"Next time it was up to $35,000.00. And before you know it I was down $50,000.00 then I was even further down owing $100,000.00. "

"I remember when the pot got up to $15,000.00. I told the guys we should quit. This is getting out of hand, we should stop this."

The rest of the players seeing all the money that could be won they said, "No!"

Thankfully, David's luck would change.

"I'm in for $100,000.00 and with my next hand I didn't take any cards. I had four books and I won the pot. Two people had to match (pay) $100,000.00. I ended up even and quit playing."

"When we arrived in Memphis, that's when the demand by the participants for payment started. Everyone was trying to make a deal."

David's only thought was, "If I lost all that money, how was I going to explain it to my wife."

Groupies

People are familiar with rock stars and their groupies. Professional athletes have them too and they can be big stars in their own right. It was a magic time in 1986. The Boston Celtics were marching through the NBA Season like "Sherman's March to the Sea." Ending up with an impressive 67 win season the Celtics were poised to go deep into the playoffs.

Their First Round Eastern Conference opponent, the Chicago Bulls and Michael Jordan went out without a whimper losing to the men from Boston three games to zero.

The Second Round would be just as impressive. Their foe was the talent-laden team from Atlanta that was led by future Hall of Famer Dominique Wilkins and future Celtics Coach Glenn "Doc" Rivers. The Celtics held off the Hawks allowing just one win to capture the Second Round series four games to one.

Moving on to the Third Round, their adversary for the Eastern Conference Finals were the Milwaukee Bucks. Well, the "Boston Massacre" continued with the Celtics once again getting out their brooms as they swept the Bucks four games to one setting themselves for the "Finals."

Having vanquished each of their opponents in the first three rounds, the Celtics were ready for the ultimate challenge-The Houston Rockets. Houston, anchored by their "Twin Towers" Ralph Sampson and

Hakeem Olajuwon, the Rockets would prove to be a very worthy opponent for the Celtics.

One phenomenon of the NBA Championship Series which culminated in a thrilling four games to two victories over the Houston Rockets was the groupies that suddenly appeared on scene. You may think I'm referring to the obvious, I am not. The groupies I am referring to are well-known professionals in their own endeavors.

All through the 1986 Championship run we started to observe some interesting people surface. Watching the U.S Open on television we saw Professional Golfer Greg Norman walking the links wearing a bright green Boston Celtics Baseball Cap. Norman we found out was a big Larry Bird fan and was a presence throughout the Celtics Playoff run.

Another famous groupie that was associated with the "Green," was Nils Lofgren guitarist for the Bruce Springsteen's E Street Band. Nils was a good friend of Celtics Forward Kevin McHale. All through that magic season whenever "The Boss" was playing in concert Lofgren could be spotted on stage wearing his friend's number thirty-two Celtics jersey. On a few occasions when the Celtics and The Springsteen Tour coincided McHale made sure his teammates secured backstage credentials and were there to watch Bruce and the band perform. One of those persons that attended the concerts was then Celtics Equipment Manager Wayne Leboux. Well for Wayne the alignment of the stars fell right into place. His job today; he is Bruce Springsteen's Road Manager and has had the privilege of being at "The Bosses'" side for quite a while now.

Kevin McHale had the unique talent of attracting some serious followers. Every summer down on Cape Cod Kevin would host a charity golf tournament at the Ocean's Edge Resort in Brewster,

Massachusetts. Guests included his Celtics teammates as well as
players and celebrities from Hollywood and around the League. For all
attendees it was a weekend of golf and other activities. There were a
couple of feel good moments that come to mind. Everybody
remembers John Minton aka Big John Studd the Wrestler. John was a
good friend of Kevin's and he participated in his tournament every
year. The celebrity golfers had to walk a gauntlet of hundreds of fans
seeking autographs in order to get on the practice tee to limber up. Big
John not only stopped to sign, he made sure that every child who
wanted to meet him and get his autograph was accommodated. It was
a classy move by a classy individual. Later in the evening VIP's were
treated to a memorable two-some. There was Charles Barkley alongside
former Boston Bruin Lyndon Byers singing an impromptu version of
"Stand by Me." Unfortunately, there is no known audio recording of
this event. After the songfest Charles' wife came up to Kevin and asked
"I hope you can control him because I can't."

Another Celtic that was into the music scene of the time was Bill
Walton "The Big Redhead." Walton's career was in its twilight when he
joined the Celtics for the 1986 season. Walton won a championship in
Portland with Doctor Jack Ramsay and, the John Wooden UCLA
product was at the end of a fourteen year stint. When he was signed by
the Celtics he was immediately accepted by his teammates. We all
scratched our heads as Bill was the counter-culture guy. He would be
seen with his private guru at Celtics Practice at Hellenic College in
Brookline. We imagined he was there just to make sure Bill was getting
the positive vibes.

All kidding aside, if McHale was a Springsteen follower it was
nothing compared to Bill Walton and his devotion to "The Grateful
Dead." With well over 600 concerts to his credit, Walton has travelled

world-wide to listen to his favorite group. There have been times when the "Big Red Deadhead" has sat in for a set on drums with the band.

I remember one evening when the Celtics were in Oakland for a game with the Warriors. A number of the Celtics Staff and players were invited to a Huey Lewis Concert. Well here's some news! After the concert ended the issue of transportation back to the team hotel surfaced. There were about six people including the Franchise himself Larry Bird. After meeting Lewis and "The News," backstage Huey offered to give Bird a ride back to the hotel. Larry to his credit asked about the rest of the guys that came with him to the show and Huey responded with a "let them get their own ride back." Larry being the good teammate told Lewis "thanks but no thanks" and rode back with the guys he came with.

Battle stations

In December of 1994, right before New Year's we were in San Antonio to play the Spurs on December 27th. The city of San Antonio was also hosting the Alamo Bowl with The Washington State Huskies playing the Baylor Bears. The night before our game a few of us headed out to the famed Riverwalk for some dinner and entertainment.

Our destination for the evening was Dick's Last Resort a gaudy, raucous place with cold beer, average food and plenty of televisions to watch whatever sports were on. After dinner we're sitting there enjoying our evening when we realized the place had filled up with people. Looking around we were surrounded by the Purple of Washington State and the Green and Gold of Baylor University. It was a perfect mix; just like throwing gasoline on a fire. After a while, the two sides were in good spirits as each group proudly sang the praises of each other's school. Mixed into the crowd now were players from both schools and everyone was having a good old time.

Our group kidded both teams with some good natured ribbing and we were all getting along splendidly for the moment. We were sitting together enjoying the good-natured camaraderie when a sweet little coed from the University of Washington walked by our table. She is wearing a very tight t-shirt sans brassiere and written on the front, "Tell me if you like my T***?" Being the red-blooded guys that we were we replied, "Yes, we do!" She giggled and ran off to join her party. Her boyfriend who just happened to be the biggest, brawniest lineman we had ever seen took offense to our response and came over to confront us.

Suddenly, chairs began to fly and we were face-to-face with a few of the Washington Huskies Football Team. Words were exchanged as we told the fellow, "Hey, if you got a problem with us responding to your girlfriend's question, she shouldn't be parading around the bar and have that t-shirt on."

I forgot to mention our party consisted of Steve Martin Charlotte Television Play-By-Play Man, Sam Russo our Vice President of Operations, Paul Manley Charlotte Coliseum Security Chief , Harold Kaufman PR Director, me and our big fellow all six foot eleven inches tall Mike Gminski my Television Analyst. Mr. Washington Huskie was looking for a battle when all of a sudden we felt this presence behind us. Somebody yelled out don't worry, we've got your back" and we turned to find most of the Baylor Bears Football Team are on our side. Just then the Manager of the joint jumped in between both sides and basically told the Washington players to "take a hike, you're in Texas now." To the cheers of the Baylor faithful and "The Eyes of Texas..." playing on the public address system we watched the Washington folks and the pretty T-shirt sulking out the door, leaving the bar and a potential ugly incident was avoided.

Shoes do make the Man

Just south of Downtown Atlanta off Peachtree Street on Mitchell Street is Friedman's Shoe Store. For over 85 years Friedman's was and is the place to go for all your personal shoe needs. While they stock most conventional sizes, the reason Friedman's was popular was it also catered to the professional athletes from all over the country and their rather large feet. Basketball, baseball, football and hockey players were regular shoppers. It was a common sight to see a charter bus unload it passengers at Freidman's for the purpose of shoe shopping. Additionally, Friedman's would always send over their van to a team's hotel and pick up any players that wanted to shop and return them back promptly to their hotel. While the first floor was for the "locals," it was the second floor that all the athletes headed for. It was there where the athletes could get style and comfort in the sizes they needed.

The second floor of Friedman's was a sanctuary for the professional athlete who with the assistance of Friedman's owner Bruce Teilhauber and his staff allowed the guys the opportunity to relax and shop without distractions.   It was a common sight to see players walk out with quite a few pairs of shoes. Whenever Canadian hockey players bought shoes they'd ask Bruce to "scuff" the soles so they could pass the shoes off as used and avoid having to pay custom duty when they returned to Canada. One place to visit at Friedman's was the Exotic Skin Room.

In there you were treated to a large selection of hand-made exotic skin shoes with a hefty price tag too. People would always ask Bruce to show them the shoes that were made for Shaquille O'Neal; they were Size 22.

I remember one time visiting Friedman's in 1988 for a late-season game against the Hawks. It was a splendid spring day so I walked the short distance from my hotel on Peachtree Street to the store. I wasn't looking for anything in particular; I was just browsing to see if anything caught my eye. I grabbed a few pairs out of the rack and sat down to try them on. Not paying much attention to who was sitting where, I sat myself down next to a gentleman also trying on shoes.

Next thing I know the owner Bruce came over to see how I'm doing. Bruce knew I was a repeat customer and he also knew I was with the Celtics. At the same time, he introduced me to the man sitting next to me.

Lew, say hello to Pete, Pete this is Lew Shuman, he's in town with the Celtics for tonight's game."

Pete was Pete Rose the former player and then current Manager of the Cincinnati Reds.

We shook hands and chatted briefly while continuing to try on shoes.

Then the conversation took a strange twist at least it did in my mind? Rose was asking me questions about the Celtics, its players and then specifically asks me whether I knew if "Bird was going to play tonight?" A little alarm went off in my head and I answered him with a brief, "I hope so!" With that our conversation ended.

Now, I don't know to this day if Rose was fishing for information. I'd like to have given him the benefit of doubt. After all, we witnessed what transpired later when Pete Rose was banned from Baseball because of gambling. It was not for me to judge whether Pete was guilty or innocent but just to disclose what was said.

The NBA is super sensitive when it comes to issue of gambling. The League has gone way beyond to protect the integrity of the game especially in light of the recent conviction of disgraced referee Tim

Donaghy. He was found guilty of betting on games and blowing his whistle to affect the outcome and point spreads of contests he had worked. Every employee working for the league and its teams now must go through stringent and continuing education on just what is acceptable conversation and what would be a violation. We are taught not to talk about injuries or if players will miss games to anyone. This game of basketball is our livelihood; and we all share with the NBA in protecting the product that we love.

Fashionable

Eddie Johnson is truly a Renaissance Man. Eddie spent 17 years toiling for six different NBA teams including the Charlotte Hornets. He was known as a go-to guy that had the ability to make the shot when it was needed. After his playing days ended, Johnson was able to capitalize on his name and fame as a professional athlete to continue his career as a gifted motivational speaker and author. His book was titled "You Big Dummy- An Athlete's "simple" Guide to a Successful Career. "

During his short tenure with the Charlotte Hornets Johnson revealed that for certain members of the Hornets their attire was something to behold. The most important detail was that they enjoyed flaunting their wardrobes.

As Eddie indicated, players like Larry Johnson, Alonzo Mourning, Johnny Newman and "Muggsy" Bogues lived to dress.

In fact, "It was a contest between these guys every day. They never wore the same thing twice and that was for 82 games. Each night a different outfit"

Folks, we were not talking about "off-the-rack" either. The guys had professional tailors at their disposal custom designing and manufacturing their suits, shirts, pants and even shoes; all to their specifications.

As Johnson had mentioned about the friendly competition,

"It got to the point that the rest of the team was asked to judge who they thought was the best dressed."

 It got so serious that one player, "Muggsy" Bogues would sit out in his car in the parking lot behind the Coliseum and wait for the other dapperly dressed players to enter before he would exit his car and make his grand entrance into the Home Locker Room."

I remember vividly just how these gentlemen looked. I recall one trip with the Hornets where we were treated to a visual spectacle of fashion by Larry Johnson, "Muggsy" Bogues and Alonzo Mourning. Larry was resplendent in a powder blue suit with matching accompaniments including shoes. "Muggsy" donned a lime green suit with corresponding trimmings while Alonzo Mourning filled his six foot ten inch frame in a plum colored suit garnished with appropriate matching frills.   While each looked splendid, walking side-by-side they resembled two and a half very tall "Fruit Loops. "

Paging Dolph Schayes

Players are always practicing their shooting skills. One of the ways that they practiced was by playing a game called H-O-R-S-E. Simply explained it's when two or more players compete by attempting and making a shot. The second player has to copy the style of the first shooter and make the same shot. If he misses he's give an "H" and the game moves forward until someone spells out H-O-R-S-E and is eliminated.

Occasionally, there would be a friendly wager placed on the game's outcome but mostly it allowed the participants a chance to loosen up and have some fun. Kevin McHale and Danny Ainge were two classic H-O-R-S-E players and most days after practice they would play. As part of their shooting repertoire they included the set-shot. Whenever they would attempt a set-shot they would yell Dolph Schayes. The "Shot" was old school basketball that was utilized in the early days of the NBA. One player who made his living from shooting the set shot was Adolph "Dolph" Schayes. Schayes played sixteen years in the NBA before moving up the bench to coach. As a player he was noted for his lethal outside shot. So in homage to Dolph, Ainge and McHale would always add the set-shot to their game of H-O-R-S-E.

Outside of the gym and usually at the airport Danny and Kevin were jokesters. As Kevin McHale declared, "we'd be dog-dead tired…flying at 5:30-6:00 in the morning and at every third airport we would jump on the airport public address system and as a joke we'd page Dolph Schayes, Dolph Schayes would you please come to Gate 13?"

This ongoing "paging" of Dolph Schayes went on for over 2 years.

Kevin went on to exclaim gleefully, "one day, I don't remember where it was but Danny had just finished paging Dolph Schayes when all of a sudden Dolph Schayes appeared at the gate and we went oh my God its Dolph Schayes and we've been paging him for two years. "

He (Dolph) asks "someone has been paging me here?"

Kevin giddily spoke to Dolph "we page you at every airport."

"Dolph thought it was so funny he sat and talked with us for over an hour."

Chapter 5

Fried Chicken and Waffles

<u>Never get off the bus</u>

Travel for today's professional athletes is nothing in comparison to how it used to be. Currently pro-athletes are treated royally compared to their brethren of years past.

Before and after every game that requires travel, they are met with a specially designed airplane to whisk them to their next destination. The interior configuration of these modern chariots would amaze the average traveler.

Teams like the Detroit Pistons, Dallas Mavericks and Portland Trailblazers with owners like Mark Cuban and Paul Allen have the deep pockets and the dollars. They own their own flying palaces to get their ballplayers from point A to point B.

The NBA and its teams now have working agreements with Delta Airlines to move their players around the country for their regularly scheduled games.

Here's where you might find it interesting.

The NBA working with Delta Airlines re-designed an Airbus Jet to accommodate its rather tall passengers. Having had the privilege of being a traveler on Flight 8942, the designated flight code for the Pelicans, I can tell you, it is the way to travel. There are three cabin sections on these planes that hold the players, coaches, team broadcasters and public relation personnel.

Every seat in two of the cabins is a first-class seat.

Every seat in the player's section is equipped with sleeper type chairs.

Comfortable plush blankets along with pillows are available for the asking.

Video screens to project game tapes or, on long-distance trips a movie.

Equipped too with Wi-Fi these planes become flying offices for its passengers.

Oh, and the food isn't too shabby either.

On an average flight a passenger can expect a multitude of appetizers served before you even buckle your seat belt for takeoff and, once you're airborne you receive a meal service that is equivalent to a five star restaurant. Passengers are treated to a variety of tasty eye appealing dishes that go the range from simple sandwiches to full course plated meals.

One very important item; Alcohol is forbidden from most NBA Charters.

Teams are responsible for their players and the last thing they want to happen is one of their players or staff getting stopped by law enforcement for a violation.

They may be cited for speeding or some other moving violation but at least they will not be cited for DUI (Driving under the Influence).

This luxurious mode of travel was not the case in the old NBA. Air travel was strictly commercial. Before charters, we travelled just like everyone else.

This relaxed travel atmosphere we knew was before the tragedy that was September 11, 2001. The resulting change in how we all travelled has created a whole generation of air travelers who have vague memories of what air travel was like before those despicable, cowardly attacks on our country.

When professional sports teams travelled pre-charters, we would all meet at the airport. We parked in the main garage and walked to the terminal and gate unlike today where we usually park on the private side of the airport in a secure lot away from the public utilizing private FBO's. These Fixed Base Operators are isolated from the main airport population and are primarily used for the private aircraft industry.

It was a common site at Boston's Logan Airport to see players like Larry Bird, Robert Parish and Kevin McHale and other Celtics wandering the shops and restaurants in the terminal before their flight was called and boarded.

Celtics Head Trainer Ray Melchiore was always there waiting at the assigned gate with tickets and boarding passes in hand. In the past everyone travelled with the team including members of the media.

Seat assignments were doled out by seniority. First-Class seats were reserved for veteran players and the head coach. The rest of us were destined for the dreaded coach section and praying we had a coveted aisle seat and not a middle seat. It was not uncommon to see a seven foot rookie or some other tall, junior player squeezed into the standard coach seat. It was not a pretty sight!

Life in the air was a little better for us when we were heading out for a West Coast trip. Chances are we'd be flying a larger airplane. We could count on flying on a Douglas DC-10 or a Lockheed L-1011; both aircraft were equipped with at least twenty-four seats in the First-Class

Cabin. Our lives would be a little more comfortable not being crammed into the Coach Section.

Being World Champions also had its advantage when we travelled on short trips.

On one visit for the Celtics, a quick in-and-out to play the New York Knicks at Madison Square Garden, it was not uncommon after the game for the Celtics to try their best to catch the last scheduled flight out of New York for Boston.

Delta Airlines, always the good partner of the Celtics would delay the departure of the last scheduled Boston flight to allow the team to make it to the airport and board without having to spend an extra night in a hotel in New York City. For the passengers sitting on the plane they were simply told it was a gate hold for some late arriving passengers.

That was where it grew interesting for me. Remember, we were flying commercially without the benefit of a luxury charter.

On this short, estimated forty-five minute flight to Boston, the best we would expect to receive as a snack was a bag of peanuts and a drink. A meal was out of the question.

So, trying to be the nice guy, I jumped off the team bus just inside Madison Square Garden and walked across 34th Street to a Kentucky Fried Chicken and ordered a large number of two-piece meals to hand out to everybody on the bus to eat before arriving at the airport.

Waiting for my order I noticed out of the corner of my eye, moving headlights and what appeared to be the team bus pulling out of its stall at the Garden and driving away. I quickly signed the credit card slip and started running down 34th Street with four shopping bags filled with fried chicken. I was left behind!

I flagged down a taxicab and told the driver, "LaGuardia Airport please." In typical New York fashion off we went. I was sure that I was going to die in a wreck covered in fried chicken while riding in a New York Yellow Cab. We were weaving in and out as we left Manhattan on our mission to get to the airport in Queens. Screaming through the Midtown Tunnel emerging into the chilly night air of Queens, we jumped on the LIE, Long Island Expressway east to the BQE, Brooklyn Queens Expressway jumping off at Exit 7 and LaGuardia Airport.

Running as hard as I could through the terminal with chicken in hand I made it to the gate and I found that our airplane was sitting at the gateway. The Ramp Agent assigned indicated it would be a late departure as we were waiting for a group that would be boarding the flight to Boston.

I started laughing and the ramp agent gave me the strangest look. Just then the team arrives. Somehow my speeding taxicab had beaten the team's charter bus to the airport.

My laughter had subsided as I sat there doing a slow burn.

First thing I did, I got up and threw the shopping bags of fried chicken into the trash. I was not going to feed a group of friends who had left me behind.

My Play-by-Play man Gil Santos came up to me and said "I tried to get them to wait but they were in a hurry not wanting to miss the flight." Even Head Coach KC Jones came up to me to apologize for leaving me behind.

Players were joking with me about watching me run down 34th Street chasing after the bus. After the laughter I told all that my motives were to benefit the team and not just myself. In the end, the lesson I learned through thirty plus years of travel with professional sports teams, never get off the bus.

Foodies

The famous quotation that "man does not live by bread alone" definitely applies to travelers; especially those who have a company credit card and expense account. I remember an early boss's firm instruction; "have a good time but don't go nuts." One of the hardships of traveling for business is that you are away from home with time on your hands. What better way to occupy one's time but to go out to eat with your associates. Dining out on an off-night on the road had become a tradition for all who traveled regularly with professional teams. There are cities we looked forward to visiting. We planned ahead of time to insure we visited the restaurants that provided us with outstanding dining opportunities and we did our best to take advantage of them. It was not unusual for a group of eight to ten individuals to head out for a night on the town. Our group contained radio and television talent, production personnel, public relations and the occasional coach or assistant coach.

While most times out we had a first-class meal, there were times that we've shaken our heads and quietly laughed. One time in Sacramento back in the mid 1980's we assembled in the lobby to head out for dinner when one of the hotel's bellman asked "Where you fellows heading tonight?" Our response was Frank Fats for Chinese Food. At the time, Sacramento was not high on the restaurant scene so we listened as the bellman gave us rave reviews for this "new Italian place" that had just opened up and everyone in Sacramento was lining up to get in and try.

Interested we asked what the name was and its location? His replied, "It's over at the Mall on Arden Way and it's called Sbarro." Not that there was nothing wrong with Sbarro. We thanked him and stayed with our plan to visit "Fats."

Imagine if you can five hungry individuals in pursuit of a meal. One night in San Francisco, it was suggested we visit a certain restaurant located in Ghirardelli Square-The Mandarin. The only minor problem was the team was staying out near the Oakland Airport and our intended destination was approximately eleven miles across the Bay Bridge in San Francisco. Add to the equation The Bay Area was being inundated by torrential rain squalls rolling in off the Pacific. The dinner party included: my television talent Gil Santos and Bob Cousy, Glenn Ordway radio voice of the Celtics, Jimmy Rodgers Assistant Coach and I. Outside our hotel lobby we grabbed a taxicab, told the driver the Embarcadero in San Francisco please and off we went into the rain drenched night.

About 30 minutes and $60.00 taxicab ride later we're in the city and we were dropped off at our destination. Then we realized that the Embarcadero is nowhere near our real destination of Ghirardelli Square. When in fact, we were two miles away from where we wanted to be. Next problem! Have you ever tried to catch a taxi in inclement weather? After a few minutes our efforts to flag down a taxi was futile. We all agreed that the only way to get there was to "hoof it." In between the squalls we headed off in the direction of Ghirardelli Square. Almost immediately the intensity of the rain increased and we extended our gait from a fast walk to a run. You could use your imagination but, the best way to describe our two mile journey of running from building to building, doorway to doorway trying to avoid the downpours was best put by Bob Cousy, "We looked like rats darting through the night" as we sought shelter at every block.

Eventually, we made it to our destination. Walking into the restaurant the hostess looks at us and asks "Is it raining?" We are all standing there soaked to the bone looking as if we just swam across San Francisco Bay. "Yes, it's raining a little bit" was our response.

For the most part the meals and service we encountered were impressive. Every once in a while we'd strike out at a restaurant. When we went out we tended to favor Italian Food, Steak or Chinese as our favorites. In most cities we visited during the regular season we knew way ahead of time where we would be dining. One game on the schedule was for the Hornets to play the Cavaliers. For many years the Cavaliers called The Richfield Coliseum home. Located about 30 miles south of Cleveland the arena was situated in the middle of nowhere. The closest town was Hinckley and yes this is the same town that was famous for the Buzzards that stopped there during their annual migration.

There were not many choices in the area for dinner especially if you were staying at the Holiday Inn right near the Coliseum, We all headed over to the nearest recommended Italian restaurant. You know the type; the one with the checkered table cloth and Chianti bottle with the melted candle wax. We were seated at a big, round table and checked out the menu which was full of the standard Italian fare that you would expect. We ordered some wine and mixed drinks and waited for the waitress to come back and take our order. Someone in our party asked the waitress, "how are the meatballs?' Without hesitation she replied, "They are fresh, the kitchen just opened the can." Like I said not all restaurants are the same.

Steve Bulpett awarded me the nick-name, "The Cruise Director..." In most cities it was left to me to make the arrangements for when and where would we go to have dinner. Over the years we all have accumulated our favorites. A few of them are still open for business and if you ever make it to them your reward will be a great meal. In no set order here are some places you're almost guaranteed to see some NBA people during the regular season.

 In Chicago we usually visited two places Gibson's or The Rosebud. Gibson's is a steak house on North Rush Street that attracts a glitzy, famous clientele. You can be sure you'll see a celebrity or athlete when you stop in. Another great place is the Rosebud on West Taylor. This Little Italy restaurant is a must visit. Bring your appetite. Their servings are huge and the food is spectacular.

Heading out to Los Angeles most teams stayed at the Ritz Carlton in Marina del Rey. Just a few short blocks away on West Washington Boulevard is the C & O Trattoria. Well-known for its outstanding breakfast menu the C & O is also an incredible eatery especially for dinner. Once you're seated the fun begins. Each patron is handed a crayon and using the honor system you draw a wheel on the paper table cloth and each spoke drawn represents a glass of wine consumed. At each place setting, you'll find a song sheet and after a few vinos everyone joined in singing the Old Italian classics. By the way the pastas served are better than Mama used to make.

When we visited Seattle before the Sonics moved to Oklahoma City Seattle seafood was king. With all the tourists heading to Pike Place Market to watch the salmon catchers, we would head the opposite direction to Seattle's Chinatown. The place we visited was The Sea Garden Restaurant. Unfortunately, this gem has closed but in its heyday it was famous for one thing Crab! You would walk up to their giant tanks loaded with live Dungeness Crabs, point at the one you want and out it comes alive and kicking. It was weighed for pricing and into the kitchen it went. A few minutes later out it came ready to eat in a phenomenal ginger, black bean sauce that was to die for. This was a twenty napkin meal as you ripped into it with your hands and you ate every last piece of crabmeat.

In Indianapolis, Indiana the home of the Pacers there is a gem of a restaurant that has become a must visit for athletes and business people alike. Serving the public since 1902 this downtown, family owned business St Elmo's has dished up the tastiest most mouth-watering steaks that money could buy. While their notoriety comes from their succulent steaks there is another item on their menu that is their main attraction. Everybody that dines at St Elmo's always starts their meal with their famous Shrimp Cocktail with "Fire." The Fire is the cocktail sauce that is served with the shrimp. Legend has it that the sauce is so hot it reminded people of St Elmo and the heat that a mighty thunderstorm's lightning discharges. Actually, it's the abundant amount of Horseradish that powers this mighty mixture that has been known to bring grown men to tears.

Rounding out our little restaurant romp I take you to my home-Boston. Always a great restaurant town Boston is known for its fresh seafood. There's a section of Boston that is walking distance from downtown called the North End. This is home to a thriving Italian neighborhood. There is a restaurant called Neptune Oyster. We like to hit this small place on Salem Street that is noted for its fresh variety of oysters on the half shell and more so it's famous for its Lobster Rolls. The Lobster Rolls are served two ways; traditional cold made with mayonnaise and hot served with real drawn butter. Either way you'll be treated to the most succulent crustacean you've ever eaten.

Its 5 degrees out there

Birmingham, Michigan in February can be bitter cold. The hotel of choice was The Townsend located right in the center of Birmingham. The hotel was convenient to Pontiac, Michigan and The Palace of

Auburn Hills where the Pistons played their home games. The restaurant of choice for the evening was Churchill's Steak House. Often when the weather was bad we opted to stay close to our hotel. We tended to order room service or casually wander into the restaurant adjacent to the lobby. But not on this night! The consensus of the group was Churchill's. No one in the group of well-seasoned travelers knew where the restaurant was located.

Bob Licht our television play-by-play man along with Gary Kirby our television director had the honor of being the point persons on where this place was and how to get there. According to the lovely lady manning the front desk Churchill's was located conveniently nearby. Bob and Gary obtained the directions and waited for the group to assemble in the lobby. Informed the restaurant was close most chose to leave their heavy winter jackets, hats and gloves in their rooms. Out the front door stepped the hearty group of broadcasters and into the misery that was a Michigan winter. Turning right they started to make their way when out of nowhere they were blasted by the wind chill that made it feel like it was well below zero when in fact it was a glacial 5 degrees.

Walking briskly at the point was Gary and Bob. The rest of the party was tagging along right behind them. Our leaders were sensing something was amiss. As they walked through the crusted ice and snow they noticed that they were leaving the commercial area in favor of a residential area. Where was Churchill's our fearless guides wondered to themselves? A few blocks turned into a half mile and no restaurant in sight. The calm of the party was deteriorating rapidly as grumbling began. They were starting to feel the effects of the bone-chilling wind and temperature. Remember, this macho group left most of their warm clothing back at the hotel. Up ahead they spotted a gas station and they ran in and confirmed what they thought; they were going the wrong way. Out of the warmth of the gas station our fearless leaders realized they made a mistake. They should have turned left out of the hotel not right. Now, instead of a brief two block walk they had to retrace their steps and travel about a mile to their destination. The group was freezing. Gary and Bob became the targets of verbal abuse, snowballs and whatever else they could hurl in their direction. The hearty group of broadcast pioneers finally made it to their destination for dinner. When they arrived a bit late for their reservation the hostess said "no problem." One request from the group, could we please sit as close to the blazing fireplace as possible?

Gattison's

Tucked away in an upscale South Charlotte Strip Mall just off Rea Road and Colony Road was a restaurant named Gattison's. This fashionable restaurant was owned by former NBA and Charlotte Hornet Player Kenny Gattison. When you look at the financial records of professional athletes it's exceedingly hard to see the successes from the failures.

We've been bombarded by the reported botched management of their individual financial holdings. We've heard about their earning enormous amounts of money only to have it squandered away. Former players like Antoine Walker, Allen Iverson and Kenny Anderson have squandered millions of dollars with nothing to show for their hard work except petitions of bankruptcy. Between the three gentlemen their estimated losses totaled in excess of $370 million dollars leaving them broke and in debt.

Success stories abound. Take for example Junior Bridgeman. Bridgeman capitalized on his twelve year career as a professional primarily with the Milwaukee Bucks by thinking ahead to securing his future after his playing days were over. Now, Bridgeman is a success story with his ownership of over 160 Wendy's Hamburger Franchises. His hard work and diligence had paid off.

Kenny Gattison was not on the corporate level of Junior Bridgeman but was his equal when it came to understanding that the future is more important when it comes to personal financial responsibilities. Asking Kenny if his venture into the restaurant business was a success? His answer was, "Yes!"

1992 was when he opened Gattison's in Charlotte. I remember a conversation I had with Kenny at his restaurant about being in the food service business and his words really stuck with me. "If you're not prepared to lose $100,000 dollars," you shouldn't be involved."

In a recent conversation with Kenny we revisited our talk about the success and failure rates of the restaurant business he candidly answered when questioned on why he opened a restaurant in the first place, "It was a relatively inexpensive venture to get into. It was an existing restaurant...so any physical changes would be minor and out-of-pocket." Kenny reminded me that he had inherited the remainder of the lease for his restaurant knowing he would be committed for at least two and half years. After the lease expired, he closed Gattison's. When questioned on why he closed it he indicated the lease had expired and, "It was an absolutely successful venture and I never lost any money. "

He further elaborated about his earlier quote about the $100,000 dollars that it was "common sense business venture 101. If you get into any business not just the restaurant business, you better have six to eight months operating capital on hand." Furthermore like all businesses outside forces directly affected the bottom line. During the summer people tended to stay away from restaurants opting to cook out at home and sales tended to drop off. If you were not totally involved you better have the right employees in place to keep a watchful eye on inventory, expenses and the cash register.   It reached the point where he could not find good people to work for him. When he closed his restaurant there were no regrets and most important; he made money out of the project.

 Gattison's business experience translated to his first-hand observations that if you wanted to be in a particular business, "you have to learn a business before you can be a business." Kenny went on to give credit to Junior Bridgeman as an example of someone who got his hands dirty first learning how to operate a business before becoming an owner.

 Talking about the wealth of current athletes Kenny reinforced, "that's the whole trick, they make a lot of money and more people are trying to get it out of their pockets…what they need to learn is to prepare for the fifty years you're going to live after you retire. Words well spoken! His advice was to find something that hold your interest and become involved as either an intern of an employee to gain the experience of running a successful business.

Arnie Ginsburg   Jerry Williams

The Author in Iran 1970

Si Rosenthal

Johnny Most   Bob Cousy   Mike Crispino

Gil Santos   Lew Shuman

Bob Licht   Gil McGregor   Steve Martin

David Stern   Lew Shuman

Gerry Vaillancourt   George Shinn

Gayle & Tom Benson

Joel Meyers Lew Shuman David Wesley

Charles Barkley   Anthony Mason   Danny Ainge

Jack Ramsay   Bill Russell   Tom Heinsohn

Bishop Keating   Kevin McHale   Robert Parish

Dick Harter   Rick Carlisle   Muggsy & LJ

Photos Courtesy: Steve Lipofsky, Lew Shuman, Layne Murdock, New Orleans Saints, New Orleans Pelicans, Charlotte Hornets, Massachusetts Broadcast Hall of Fame, Music Museum of New England and The Diocese of Northern Virginia.

Chapter 6

The Hall of Fame and Me

<u>School Days</u>

Being part of the Celtics entourage as well as my other teams was exciting. You were lucky to have the opportunity to associate with a large number of former players and current Hall of Fame members.

To date there are thirty-three former Celtics that have been enshrined in the Hall of Fame in Springfield, Massachusetts. Coaches, players and team administrators all are deserving members of the Hall of Fame.

Visiting teams playing in the Boston Garden were reminded of this achievement every time they looked up at the rafters and saw the banners hanging down that identified players that were enshrined and some with their numbers permanently retired. Up there too were the banners that signified the number of championships won.

There are seventeen banners hanging in the Boston Garden including an un-equaled run of eight championships in a row during the late 1950's and early 1960's.

Being a part of this mystique required some double-duty on my behalf. As I had mentioned, college for me after high school was not in the picture. After maturing a bit, I came to the reality while it was nice being a high school graduate, it would be nicer to be a college graduate.

I enrolled at the University of Massachusetts Harbor Campus in Boston and I attended classes mornings and evenings earning my degree after an eight year battle to balance work, school and personal life.

As my collegiate career neared its finale, senior semester courses taken were less intense and more casual.

What better course was there to attend and pick up a quick three credits then Coaching Basketball?

Walking into the gym that first day I kind of expected the reception I would receive. The teacher/coach was former Celtic great and fans favorite Jim Loscutoff.

I was treated no different than any of the other student attending his course. It was both a classroom and gymnasium based curriculum. There would be one difference; Professor Loscutoff was aware of who I was and what I did. For me to be absent it was because I was travelling with the team. When I returned to class it was not X's and O's that I had to report on but the previous night's game and present from a coach's perspective just how and why the Celtics won or lost the game? If Professor Jim felt I had adequately supported my theory then I earned a passing grade on the test that was given to the other students that were in the class. At the end of the semester I earned my three credits.

Bill Russell

As the Team's television producer and director I had the opportunity to encounter and mix with all the old time players and coaches. Meeting other Celtic hall of famers didn't always have that warm and fuzzy effect on the road. This was to be the case when I visited Philadelphia. Philadelphia is known for its rowdy fans. Even their hockey team was called the "Broad Street Bullies."

You have to understand that the Philadelphia sports fans are some of the most rabid in the world. One time during the Christmas season, viewers watching on television witnessed Santa Claus duking it out in the stands. Sometimes the action spilled out onto the court. Playing in Philadelphia was always an adventure. There was a fierce rivalry between Boston and Philadelphia. Tempers simmered as both teams started the 1984-1985 Season. An early November game was on the schedule and both teams were eager to have at each other. Even Johnny Most was into it telling his audience that he was high above courtside in "the city of brotherly hate-Philadelphia."

On that chilly November night in 1984 with the Celtics at the Spectrum, a fight broke out between two big super stars. Late in the third quarter a clearly frustrated "Doctor" Julius Erving ran at Larry Bird and connected with a punch to his head. Benches cleared as players stormed the court to defend each other's turf. After peace was restored, the game continued and finished with a Celtic win.

That would be the atmosphere the next time we played in Philadelphia. Coincidently Bill Russell was scheduled to work that game as an analyst for Turner Sports. Playing in Philadelphia that night turned out to be a quiet affair. The only distraction of any kind was a light fixture that was hanging precariously over the Turner announcer position. After that was taken care of the visiting Celtics went on to beat the 76ers in their own home.

It is tradition after every game home or away players and coaches usually head out for a post-game meal to socialize and discuss the game that was just played. Win or lose this ritual continues to this day. In addition to my duties as producer and director, being the rookie on the broadcast crew I was also the driver of the rental car that we used. We headed back to our hotel.

Bob Cousy and I rode up the elevator to drop our bags off in our rooms before we headed down for the post-game meal. I threw my stuff in my room, freshened up a bit and headed back down to the restaurant.

As I walked in "The Cooz," signaled me to come on over. I joined him at the table where he was not alone.

Sitting down to my left was KC Jones Head Coach of the Boston Celtics.

Across from me was Bob Cousy.

And to my right is Celtic Number 6, William Felton Russell.

For a hoop junky like me this was Nirvana.

Not only am I sitting with three retired NBA players, I'm sitting with three members of the Naismith Basketball Hall of Fame who combined have in their possession 28 World Championships and the same number of rings to go with them .

Most times you can't get me to shut up but sitting there I had nothing to say. We had dinner they talked and I listened. I witnessed three gentlemen expressing a love for each other and a game called basketball. After dinner I excused myself. I was on a mission! Up in my room was a copy of Bill Russell's new book: "Russell Rules." I grabbed the book, ran back to the restaurant and sat down. For those of you who know Bill Russell he never signed an autograph for anyone. I casually picked my spot and asked respectfully, "Bill would you please autograph your book for me?" The response I received was the classic response that I've seen him give people requesting his autograph a hundred times before, a simple "I don't sign." Pulling the book back I sat there rejected. Then the other members of the party piped in.

First it's KC Jones telling Russell "why can't you sign the kid's book?'

Jones goes on to say, "You know him he's not a stranger."

Then Cousy added his two cents. "Russ." He always called him Russ.

"Come on sign the guy's book, he's family." But, Bill Russell stood firm!

A little dejected yes, but hey, I got over it.

Well, you should all know that:

a) The Celtics won that game against Philadelphia that night.

b) The Celtics in 1986 eventually became one of the best teams in the history of the NBA.

c) And Bill Russell never signed my Book.

As a footnote, on how times change. Now, Russell sees the financial reward that could be gained by simply signing "Bill Russell." He now signs a limited amount of autographs and merchandise.

Father Dick

One of the benefits of travelling with a professional sports team is that once in a while depending on the length of the trip and the cities visited our wives would make the trip with us or join us in the middle of a long road trip.

In the NBA, there are cities you can't wait to visit and there are the ones that Doug Moe the former player and coach would refer to as "dogs." We all looked forward to visiting New York City, Seattle, Los Angeles but we were not very fond of certain cities in the dead of winter. New Jersey, Cleveland and Detroit in the winter were colorless gray and not at the top of our list.

We loved going to Washington DC home of the then called Washington Bullets. The City had its historical significance as well as some decent dining establishments. Playing in the Capital Center which later became the US Airways Arena was always a treat. In an era before big-bang halftime entertainment The Capital Center's entertainment consisted of Tiny One a miniature dachshund that when released by its owner, Building Supervisor, George Gentry, would run the entire length of the court pulling a tiny covered wagon.

The Capital Center was also the home of the loudest, antagonistic heckler that ever attended an NBA game; Robin Ficker. Ficker was a lawyer by trade and with his obnoxious mouth he sat directly behind the visiting team's bench. His constant verbiage bordered on hostile and insulting but it was usually ignored by most players who would in return just glare at him or smile.

He came armed every night. I remember one evening when the 76ers were playing and Ficker spent the entire game railing on Charles Barkley. Holding Barkley's book in his hand he screamed, "Charles, Charles how can you be misquoted in your own biography, you wrote it." This conduct applied to every superstar that visited the D.C. area. No one was spared a tongue lashing from Ficker.

So, on this particular trip, I was with the Celtics and my wife Sharyn had joined me for the trip. Bob Cousy let it be known that after the game we'd be joining some friends of his at a restaurant that one of them had a small ownership percentage. We would be meeting his friend Ken Haggarty a Washington DC dentist and teammate of Cousy's from Holy Cross where both were members of the 1947 NCAA Championship Team and a priest from the Washington area that Bob was friendly with.   Cousy and Haggarty along with their associates from Holy Cross were solid practicing Catholics. Even when we were travelling Cousy would get up early on Sunday mornings and head out to the nearest Roman Catholic Church for Sunday Mass. No matter where we were, he made sure he attended church. So it was not unusual for Bob to arrange for his friend, Ken and the "Good Father" to have tickets left for them at the arena's Will-Call window.

After the game my wife and I came inside the arena and we met up with Bob, Ken and the priest. Cousy with his dry wit introduced us to Ken and Dick the priest as "my little Jewish friend and his wife Sharyn." We shook hands and made some small talk. I had the rental car so play-by-play man Gil Santos, my wife and I headed out to the restaurant for a little late-night dinner.

We arrived at the restaurant and we sat down and relaxed with a round of beverages. Ken disappeared into the kitchen to place our orders and came back to join us. At this time, another younger priest came in and joined our group and he sat at the other end of the table talking to Ken, Gil Santos and Cousy. Sharyn and I were talking to Father Dick. Father Dick appeared to be in his mid-fifties. Dressed in plain chinos, plaid shirt with his ecumenical collar visible along with a baseball cap Father Dick was simply enjoying a night out with friends.

We continued talking over dinner and drinks discussing just about everything; politics, religion, inter-faith cooperation between Catholics and Jews; you name it we discussed it.

As the evening began to wrap-up, my curiosity peaked when I simply asked Father Dick in a rather casual tone, "Dick, tell me where your Parish is?"

Father Dick replied with one word, "Virginia!"

A little naïve and not understanding, I remember saying, "Excuse me, did you say Virginia?"

He smiled and gave us a little wink.

It seems we had the pleasure of meeting and dining with Archbishop John Richard Keating of the Northern Virginia Archdiocese.

And on future occasions when we visited the District, we'd see our friend Father Dick Keating at Bullets games where he had the opportunity to cheer with the rest of the crowd.

Dirty Lew

In the mid-1980's television was without charge and very little else compared to what we have available to us today. Back then there was over-the-air television, ESPN and Turner aka TNT. There was no NBA League Pass no Direct TV or Dish Network. Basketball broadcasts were limited to a game a week after the first of the year on CBS (1983-1989) and TNT (1988). Each team had their own "rights" deal with a local television station to televise their games. Technically, the games were delivered to the television stations one of two ways; either by AT & T land-based microwave or via the newer technology of Satellite distribution. C-Band was the accepted method for satellite transmission and reception.

For many people in America, the only way they could receive games along with other programming was by installing a satellite dish receiver in their yards or on their roofs. Transmission and reception was not as sophisticated as is today. The technology of Direct TV and Dish Network has made the 1980's acquisition of programs for home viewing archaic and primitive. All over the country giant C-Band receiving dishes sprouted up. Often referred to as "West Virginia State

Flowers," these huge 12 foot dishes dotted the landscape. With these receivers people were now capable of tuning in and watching a myriad of programming especially sports. Early on most satellite transmitted programming was free. With this free programming came something I had never experienced; my own personal group of fans. How did I gain this notoriety and appreciation; here's how?

Whenever there was an appropriate stoppage in game action we were allowed to take our commercial breaks. By doing so we sent it back to our station where they ran the commercials that you watched. For 1:30 to 2:00 we had a break on-site waiting for the station to return to us for the game to continue. To fill time our camera operators would search the crowd for interesting people. Most of the time, they would end up shooting the dancers, cheerleaders or attractive female fans in the stands. Sometimes the camera lens would get a bit too tight or they would capture a certain part of the anatomy. What we tended to forget was that anyone who was watching on satellite was also seeing what we were seeing in the mobile unit. Almost immediately I was receiving fan mail, cards and letters on what a great job I was doing covering the games especially when we went to commercials. I was receiving correspondence from all over the Western Hemisphere from sports bars, military bases and regular viewers all encouraging me to continue to feed the great content that was going out on the satellite. Mind you, this was only seen by people who had the ability to receive the signal via satellite downlinking. No one in our television market was seeing what the satellite world was seeing. It almost reached cult hero status for me. I remember one time when Bob Cousy was guesting on a Dallas Radio program when the host Norm Hitzges asked him, "Who is Dirty Lew?" Cousy went on to explain our little video voyeurism to him.

I started to receive correspondence from a Sports Bar in San Leandro, California. It was called Ricky's. Owned by a gentleman named Ricky

Ricardo I was extended an invitation for the next time we were in Golden State to stop by and be his guest. Though I was dubious, the next time we were in Oakland to play we all trekked over to check out Ricky's. Still the skeptic, I thought we were all crazy to visit this place and I was glad we went as a group.

Ricky's was located in a strip mall on Hesperian Boulevard in San Leandro, California just down the road from Oakland.

We walked in! And the hostess asked, "How many?"

I responded, "Is Ricky around?"

Just than from behind the bar this guy bounced out to greet us. In a moment he realized who we were. He had recognized Gil Santos and Bob Cousy from our broadcasts.

He cries out, "It's them, it's them. Which one of you is Lew?"

I wave shyly and he ran over to shake my hand. He told the hostess, "take care of them and give them anything they want."

We went on to have a delightful evening eating, sipping and watching hoops on his many televisions. In fact, Ricky's turned out to be a great friend and find for future visits to the Bay area. Ricky's was the precursor and prototype of what the classic sports bar has become. If you happen to stop in, be sure to ask Ricky to show you my picture, it should still be up on his "Wall of Fame."

The Fourth Estate

There's a word in Yiddish that is used to describe a good, kind individual; a "Mensch." During my two seasons associated with The Philadelphia 76ers I had the honor and opportunity to know and work with a real Mensch-Phil Jasner.

I had moved on from the Celtics and was producing and directing the 76ers road telecasts. It is there where I met and became a friend of Phil Jasner. He was a writer for the Philadelphia Daily News. Often we would get together for dinner in whatever city we happened to be in and spend the evening talking about one or two of our favorite subjects the NBA and the Sixers. It was the 1992-1993 season and Philadelphia had unloaded Charles Barkley to The Phoenix Suns for veterans Jeff Hornacek , Tim Perry and Andrew Lang. This edition of the Sixers was high on talent but was lacking the cohesion to put away opponents on a regular basis.

One night in February, Phil and I had made arrangements to meet for dinner in Charlotte, North Carolina and catch the Sixers at Atlanta game on television. Scheduled to play a back-to-back against the Hornets the next night we headed for a sports bar on East Independence Drive called The Scoreboard where we settled in to watch some hoops, have dinner and relax. What we sat through was a massacre. The Sixers were destroyed by the Hawks 132 to 107. The Sixers team we just watched was not good and we just witnessed why; they could not hit a shot! We always talk about irony in sports. Well the irony was on the television screen right after the game.

The game goes off the air and we're treated to an infomercial on how to improve your basketball shooting skills called "The Shot Doctor!" It featured Sixer Shooting Guard Hersey Hawkins and the current Sixer Assistant Coach Buzz Braman. It was a half hour of instruction how to do nothing but shoot the basketball. Something the 76ers had failed to do that very evening in Atlanta. Phil and I were rolling with laughter and I can tell he's starting to get an idea for his next story in The Philadelphia Daily News. Hey Folks, how about buying a video for people who can't shoot from people who can't shoot? Phil was a gem of a man who loved to cover basketball.

I would see Phil whenever he'd travel to New Orleans to cover the Sixers and the Hornets. Phil also knew that my wife and I were having trouble finding good bagels in New Orleans. While "The Big Easy" may have some of the best food in the world there were some things lacking and bagels was one of them. He did not have to, but Phil was kind enough to bring us a dozen, fresh assorted bagels which he had picked up earlier in the day on his way to the airport and hand-delivered them to us. Phil you were a Mensch and you were a friend! Sadly, we lost Phil to cancer in December of 2010 at the age of 68. His passing was a tremendous loss to his family, his readers, his peers and the sports world that he covered for nearly 30 years.

Every sports team has press coverage. The Media that are usually assigned to report on them daily are the beat writers of the Fourth Estate. Depending on the number of newspapers in the team's hometown, the number of reporters that travel could be as low as one reporter or for a major market like New York it could be as many as five. When I was working in Boston, we had four regular writers assigned: Steve Bulpett represented the Boston Herald, Mike Fine was with the Quincy Patriot Ledger and the Boston Globe alternated Bob Ryan, Jackie MacMullan, and Dan Shaughnessy. Peter May from the Hartford Courant was the fourth. They were not immune to the occasional mischief that was always around a large traveling group. During one extended road trip with the Celtics we decided to celebrate Mike Fine's birthday, except we had determined that his birthday would be every day of the road trip. Whenever we went out to dinner we made sure there was a cake with candles and our voices singing happy birthday to Mike. Fine had to leave the road just before the last game was to be played but that didn't stop us. On the last television broadcast of the trip, Gil Santos and Bob Cousy made sure they wished Mike Fine a very happy birthday from all his friends with the Celtics.

Steve Bulpett of the Boston Herald reminded me of the time when we were at National Airport preparing to leave for another road game. Steve who measures in at about six foot four inches and could pass for a basketball player was sitting in the departure area with the six foot one Celtic Sam Vincent. Vincent was drafted by the Celtics in 1985 and played two seasons with Boston before departing for Seattle and Chicago. While with Boston, Vincent was a part of the 1986 Championship Team. Both Bulpett and Vincent were in a casual conversation when a well-dressed lady approached Steve and asked, "Are you a basketball player, can I have your autograph?" Steve graciously thanked her and explained, "No ma'am, I am not a basketball player." The lady then turned to Vincent and inquired, "Do you play?" Vincent's replay was, "hardly ever." With his answer you knew his time in Boston was limited.

Ready one, Take two

When working a game the Director expects the crew to be prepared. This is most important for the camera operators assigned to the game. We expect them to do their homework on the teams that they will be shooting. Not to say that the director is innocent but both need to be prepared. Sitting in a mobile unit game after game there were some humorous moments. That's why most directors hand out contact sheets with the pictures of each team's player and coaches. I remember one incident in Charlotte a few years back involving one of my camera operators. Usually after the opening talent standup and player introductions most broadcasts then do the starting lineups followed by a commercial break. Upon returning from the commercial break the game starts with the opening tip off. Prior to the tip most directors fill the short time with faces (players). They like to get nice close-ups of the players heading for center court to fill time up leading up to the ball toss. On this particular night I was faced with about thirty seconds to fill prior to the start of the game.

I instructed my tight camera to "shoot faces." Not seeing a response from the camera I again instructed the operator, "2- I'm looking for faces. Help me out."

All my other cameras were doing what I asked with one exception; my high tight camera operator was lost. Then on my headset I hear my tight camera operator open his talk key and he asks "faces, what are faces?"

I responded sarcastically, "Faces…it's the front part of the head where their noses are hanging." The camera person realized what I wanted and began to shoot the players. It seemed I had taken for granted that this particular camera person was familiar with the jargon that I used.

Once when I first started directing I remember we were doing a Boston College Eagles football game from Alumni Stadium in Chestnut Hill, Massachusetts. It was clear that in addition to my being new as a director it was obvious that the technical crew was new at doing sports remotes. I have a saying for folks that do not do remote broadcasts on a regular basis. They are called S-P-O-R which translates to studio people on remote. This is not to put them down but these folks traditionally do their work in a studio environment with little field experience. Add to the mix a lack of knowledge of sports in general and it can lead to some funny happenings. We were doing this football game and all of us were studio people attempting to do a live event outside of our comfort zone. We had just gone on-the-air and it was moving along reasonably well when I asked one of my camera operators Marcy Paul to get a shot of the head coach of the Eagles Ed Chlebek. Marcy immediately clicked on her headset and asked. "What's his number?" Even today whenever we talk, we laugh and remind each other of this classic moment.

Another mix-up of words that can be disastrous to a broadcast is when the director and the technical director are not on the same page. The word "ready" is the most important word used followed by the word "standby" when working in a mobile unit. Standby gets everyone's attention that something is about to happen. And "ready" means a command was given and is about to be executed. Following attentively are your crew especially your technical director and audio mixer. They control what the viewer will see and hear. In a normal situation you would hear the following as a broadcast went on-the-air.

"Standby, we are live in thirty seconds…Ready to roll open and track playback on X." The countdown continues "5, 4, 3, 2, 1 roll X track X fade up on X" and off you go for two and half to three hours of live television. Another key word for all in the crew is anticipate. Most experienced operators can think one step ahead of the director and most of the times they have a good sense as to what will be happening next. Here's where it can get tricky. The director is watching multiple monitors to keep track of the game.

It is a constant chatter of "ready one, take one, two bring in the substitution, ready two, take two. Let's look at the replay, who has it? Y? Ready Y, roll Y, wipe to Y. Two get me number 24 he committed the foul, wipe to two and so it goes. The worst call a director can make is "ready one-take two." You better pray your technical director is paying attention. If not you're going to a camera that is not ready and shooting who knows what. I've had many TD's save my butt by uttering three words. "Are you sure?"

Chapter 7

You can't make this stuff up

<u>Charles Barkley</u>

Of all the teams and individuals that I traveled with none was more fun to be around then "Sir Charles" aka Charles Barkley. Barkley was from Leeds, Alabama via Auburn University. Charles can be best described as an enigma. If you understand the "Chuckster" you are way ahead of the game-his game.

Drafted by the Philadelphia 76ers in 1984 the "Round Mound of Rebound" had an immediate effect on the game. As a player he was a fierce competitor and his rebounding skills were his stock in trade.

Charles was known for his irreverent behavior. Once at a game he was being heckled by a cretin who was uttering racial slurs in his direction. Charles exploded, turning toward his heckler he spat at him and missed his intended target and ended up spitting on a young girl sitting nearby. Heavily fined for this incident, Charles later apologized to the little girl and her family.

Charles in his younger days had this habit of turning into a trouble magnet. One time in Milwaukee, Charles took offense to an antagonist who came at him with a balled fist and punished the offender by punching him and breaking his nose. The following morning while we were on the team bus waiting to head for the airport, one of the players yelled out "Where's Charles"? Then Head Coach Jim Lynam turned and replied, "Charles will not be joining us, Let's Go!" We later found out that Charles had been arrested by the Milwaukee Police and was waiting to be arraigned.

Charles by the way, you still owe me five dollars that you borrowed to "grease" the Maître D's pocket for a good table in Chicago.

Armon Gilliam

Charles always liked to poke fun at his teammates. One player that drove him completely crazy was the late, Armon Gilliam. Armon was nicknamed "The Hammer" for his huge arms and his intense play under the basket. Gilliam was a thirteen year veteran of the NBA. Drafted by the Phoenix Suns, he travelled around the league playing for Charlotte, Philadelphia, New Jersey, Milwaukee and Utah. I knew Armon to be one of the quietest, gentlest individuals in basketball.

His quietness drove Charles crazy. There were times that Charles wanted Armon to retaliate after being fouled hard, but Gilliam just shook it off and continued to play his game.

Ever the joker, Charlie did his best to bait Armon whenever he could and Gilliam would quietly sit back and ignore him.

Every team and its players follow pretty much the same game-day rituals. They start the day with a Shoot-Around either at their home arena or the venue they will be playing in on the road. Lasting an hour in length, it's where the head coach lays out the plan for that evening's game. At this shoot-around/walk-thru, the team practices and "walks through" the plays it will execute and they will practice defending their opponent.

After that the players are pretty much on their own until they have to report for the actual game. Some players linger to get treatment from the Head Trainer while most players spend their time resting, eating light and getting their mind-set for the upcoming contest. When they arrive at the arena, they change into their warm-ups, head out onto the court to shoot, loosen up and return to the locker room.

Each player prepares in his own way. Some quietly stretch to loosen and limber up their muscles. Others with headsets on listen to music. Eventually, the players change from their warm-ups to their game uniforms before receiving a final chalkboard talk from the coach.

Armon Gilliam was no different. His mode of relaxation and concentration was to read.   He was a prolific reader and a book at his side was his way of getting ready for the game that was about to be played. This particular night, it would be his chance to put Charles gently in his place.

Charles walked into the Sixers locker room and scanned the scene. He spots Armon quietly sitting in front of his locker deep into the book he was reading.

Charles took his shot!

"Armon, Armon what's that in your hand?"

Gilliam ignores Charles.

Charles again baits Gilliam. "What's that?"

Gilliam frustrated by the interruption of his private time looks up from in front of his locker and looks at Charles and with his deep booming voice delivers his retort,

"Charles, this is a book and it's something you've never seen or held in your life."

Well, the pre-game tension in the locker room dissolved as the laughter drowned out Charles' mumbling resulting in Gilliam scoring a knock-out of his teammate. The last word went to Gilliam.

Charles on the Tour

With a rare day off in Sacramento from broadcasting the 76ers in the early 1990's I had the opportunity to play a round of golf with Charles Barkley. At this time in his career Charles had yet to master the art of "hitting the pill." Every item in Charles' golf repertoire to say the least was missing. His tee shot was absent of any form. His putting resembled a croquet mallet striking a ball. And his chipping and sand play was non-existent. If you were to assign Charles a handicap it would have to be his clubs.

Charles like the rest of the golfing world takes their game and the frustration that comes with it quite seriously. The Concierge at our hotel the Hyatt Regency in Sacramento graciously arranged for our twosome to play at a nearby public course, I met Charles as he was getting off the team bus after practice and we headed out to the course at Haggin Oaks.

When we arrived at the Pro Shop the Course Pro provided us with a set of clubs, cart and a couple of sleeves of balls. From parking our rental car to the time we entered the Pro Shop the news spread like wildfire that a certain, large NBA player was on site and about to tee off.

Golfers started appearing from everywhere and Charles loved the attention. Suddenly and willingly Charles had transformed into Al Czervik the Rodney Dangerfield character from the movie "Caddyshack." He was genuinely friendly, talkative and generous to the other golfers; offering some a sleeve of balls or to another a hat with the course's logo printed on it. He was working the room and loving it. We paid our fee and off we went to conquer the "mighty eighteen."

Hole after hole Par 4, 5 or Par 3 it did not matter to Charles. He was slicing and dicing his way with double and triple bogeys all the while casting divots the size of small children. We were expecting a gallery following equal to "Palmer" but we were pretty much left to ourselves. The other golfers left us alone except for the occasional donation of extra golf balls to replace the ones that we had lost forever in the near bye rough or had drowned in the adjacent water hazards.

After our round, we dropped our bags along with our cart back at the Pro Shop. Charles graciously signed autographs and joked with the patrons. I'll give Charles credit. He has taken the time to improve his game. He may still have that huge hitch in his backswing but his game has softened and he's playing a better game of golf. Just ask him!

Manute Bol

Another Charles Barkley running buddy was Sixer Manute Bol. Manute was a product of the Sudan and member of the Dinka Tribe. He was at the time the tallest player in the league measuring in at 7 feet 7 inches. One year, Manute was teamed with Muggsy Bogues who measured in at 5 foot 3 inches. For that season with the Washington Bullets Bogues and Bol were the shortest and tallest players on the same team in the NBA.

To those who knew him Manute was the skinniest and funniest person in the NBA. Along with his seven foot frame, Bol had the longest fingers of any man alive. I've never seen hands and fingers that long. What everyone who ever knew Manute have all said was they always tried to stay next to him never directly in front of him? Why? Pity the poor person who stood in front of Manute on an elevator, stairs, bus, airplane or escalator.   If he knew who you were watch out you would be the recipient of his finger. Being the joker, Manute was constantly "goosing" whoever was in the range of his extra-long digits.

ID Please

In their 7th NBA Season, the 1994-1995 Hornets were the talk of the town. Charlotte, North Carolina and the Charlotte Coliseum was the hotbed for NBA action in the Carolinas.

Their sell-out streak (364) was continuing and their eye-popping purple and teal merchandise was jumping off the shelves to lead the entire league in merchandise sales.

The 1994-1995 Charlotte Hornets earned their second best ever overall record of 50 wins and 32 losses. Under the command of Head Coach, Allen Bristow, the Hornets roster included: fan-favorite Tyrone "Muggsy" Bogues, "Grand Mama "Larry Johnson, Alonzo Mourning and a host of veteran players like Robert Parish, Hersey Hawkins, Michael Adams and super shooter Dell Curry. Dell is the father of Stephan Curry of the Golden State Warriors. They helped fill out a very deep and talented squad.

Despite their regular season record, The Hornets witnessed defeat early on losing three games to one at the hands of a Michael Jordan led Chicago Bulls team in the First Round of the NBA Playoffs.

On that roster was an affable youngster and former Kansas Jayhawk Darrin Hancock. Fresh from a cup of coffee with the Pro League in France Hornets Director of Player Personnel Dave Twardzik let everyone know in the Hornets camp that he had seen Darrin play at the annual pre-draft camp that was held every year in Chicago and according to Twardzik, "he can flat-out run the floor..."

So, Darrin Hancock became a member of the Charlotte Hornets.

The rigors of an 82 game NBA season can wear on a player. Practice, travel and game times have to all be managed by each player in their own way. Being late was a fineable offense and violating team rules was punishable again by being assessed a monetary figure that eventually made it to a supporting employee as a thank you or it was turned over to a charity as a donation.

Early in the season Darrin, it appeared somehow lost his identification.

Well, how would a professional athlete with no formal identification in their possession, get around the possibility of being stopped by the police and not being able to prove who he really is?

Well the opportunity to put it to work happened on the team's first trip out of the country to play the Raptors in Toronto.

Remember, this is 1995 and long before the terror attacks of 9/11. Travelling was not as strict as we know it to be today. Faced with the dilemma of how we were going to get Darrin cleared though Canadian Customs and into Canada it required creativity.

Our quick thinking Head Trainer, Terry Kofler had an idea and presented it to Hancock. Unlike the commercial side of the airport, charter aircraft always taxied to the private general aviation side of the airport and customs officials would board the plane, check for contraband and identification and then clear the aircraft and passengers to disembark.

Sitting on the plane we waited for Customs to do their due diligence.

One-by-one we showed our ID's. Some of us used our passports while others used their driver's licenses which were allowed at the time. Well, the Customs Official walked up to Darrin and he asked for identification. Without skipping a beat, Darrin opened the team's 1995-1996 Media Guide to page 61 and hands it over to the Customs Official and says, "That's me!"

Very slowly and skeptically the official looks at Darrin and again looks at the Media Guide. He smiled, shaked his head on moved on.

For the first time in history of organized professional sports a team's Media Guide was used for identification.

In fact, Darrin spent the rest of the season with the Media Guide at his side at all times.

Duck

The Celtics were in Atlanta for a game against the Hawks. Before Phillips Arena opened the Hawks played at The Omni. A dingy dark avant-garde looking venue; it was not a great building for fans or broadcasters. The mobile units were parked in the rear of the Omni facing the adjacent railroad yard. We were distracted by our senses; especially smell. Our broadcast trucks were always aligned next to the main dumpsters that handled all of the building's waste. When it was cold it smelled and, when it was warm it really smelled.

You should know that for an arena to be profitable, it needs to take advantage of all "bankable dates." That means a constant flow of sports, concerts and live events are essential to their financial viability. You need at least one hundred scheduled events per year to turn a profit.

It is a very common occurrence for a concert to be booked one night and the next night host a sporting event. That was the case when we were in Atlanta. While the building was being converted from three rings to the hardwood, all the circus' support vehicles and animals were stored outside the arena next to where we parked.

Every good director has a camera meeting with his camera operators before going on-the-air. At this get together the director hands out a contact sheet with the head shots of players and coaches from both teams. He will go over team strengths and weaknesses and he will lay out how he would like his cameras to perform.

For this meeting I decided to gather outside the mobile unit for our camera meeting and then take a scheduled meal break. Here we are all together in a group and we're talking about our preparation for the upcoming game. We were not paying too much attention of what was going on around us. All of a sudden and out of nowhere a cage being pulled by a circus roustabout passed right in front of us. Before we can move its occupant, a full-grown stunning Bengal tiger proceeded to spray us from inside its cage with a long large trail of urine. We had nowhere to go-we were sitting ducks! I have to tell you tiger urine stinks. It smells even more when it on your clothes and you're confined to a really small compact area like the inside of a television mobile unit.

The camera people were lucky; they were able to be inside the building at their camera positions with the smell confined to them. Unfortunately for me when I returned to the television truck the odor permeated the entire unit for the evening. So, for those of you who think television is a glamorous life; it can be as long as you're not urinated on by a tiger.

It's just Anita!

There are 30 teams in the NBA and there are an equal number of television producers and directors that handle their respective team's broadcasts. You can say that we're members of an exclusive fraternity and we all know each other.   There are 2,460 regular season games played and we meet on a regular basis. With our steady get-togethers we feel a kindred spirit toward our friends that do the same job that we do 82 plus times a year. You should know your job is hard enough to execute at home compared to the added difficulties in producing a game on the road with an unfamiliar crew, mobile unit. Factoring in weather; they all affect your performance.

As a Director of Broadcasting and a former producer and director I made sure that when one of my peers shows up in my town I would go out of my way to make them feel welcome when they arrived on site. I tried to satisfy any production needs they might have. Production requests vary from a simple game footage request highlighting one of our players to finding them a great place to eat after the game; that's my version of television customer service. I treated my visitor the way I would want to be treated when I visited his or her city. After all, I wore their shoes for at least 25 years.

Most requests are simple with minimal difficulty. Once in a great while we go above and beyond to help an associate. Howie Singer the Director for the New York Knicks gave me a call. Howie has been a colleague for many years. Working as a "road warrior" for most of his career he has had his share of unusual happenings. One time in Charlotte while doing a game he asked his runner to please, get him some water. Now, the written rule is no open containers of any kind are allowed in a mobile unit. After all, water and electronic equipment do not mix. Eager to be helpful, the young runner quickly returned with a cup of iced water. In his haste as he was passing the cup to Howie, he tripped and dumped the entire open cup of H2O on to Howie and his video switcher instantly shorting it out taking them off the air. After some quick re-wiring by the trucks EIC (Engineer in Charge) with the assistance from my home broadcast Howie was able to continue his show utilizing my show's cameras sans graphics using a back-up router to switch his game. So, when he called later in the season requesting a favor to do some video editing for our game on Monday night asking if I could help, I responded to the affirmative. I mentioned to Howie that he would have to come down to the Hornets Training Facility where our editing bays were located.

The Hornets played at the Charlotte Coliseum in Charlotte North Carolina and they practiced at The Hornets Training Facility in Fort Mill, South Carolina about thirteen miles south of the Coliseum. In fact the Charlotte city limits ends at the South Carolina border. I gave Howie directions on how to get to the training facility from his hotel in the Southpark section of Charlotte.

It was an estimated 15-20 minute drive on a Sunday. All he had to do was take Tyvola Road back toward the Coliseum, jump on Interstate 85 South and get off at the Tega Cay/Knights Stadium Exit and up Gold Hill Road that would lead him to the training facility located adjacent to the Charlotte Knights AAA Baseball Team's ballpark. He would be met by an editor around 2pm who would let him into the facility and he could do what he needed to do.

Now, Howie is a full-blooded New Yorker. In the concrete jungle that is Manhattan, Howie's world is people moving at a fast pace while ignoring everyone around them. It's the big city! Now, he's heading into rural South Carolina and on a Sunday. Not quite sure if he's in the right place Howie pulls into the only business open on Gold Hill Road the neighborhood convenience store; The One-Stop. The store was atypical of the rural South. Signs advertising Cold Beer, Lottery Tickets and Fresh Boiled Peanuts were on display to tempt the local population. At the edge of the driveway was a sign with "Stop by and say hello to Anita." All surrounded and under the watchful flags of both the "Stars and Stripes and the Stars and Bars." Howie found the only telephone booth on the property and gave me a call unsure of whether he was in the right place?

The phone rang my wife answered. "There's a Howie on the Phone."

I picked it up and said "Hey, what's up?

I re-assured Howie that he just needed to turn right after the convenience store head up the winding road a bit and he'd be at the training facility.

All of a sudden Howie sensed something or someone is watching him. Without warning Howie shouted into the phone, "There's a pig here and its right in front of me." I'm not talking a little pig this is a big one."

Howie, I said, "It's just Anita." She won't bother you; she's just looking for a snack." Howie said goodbye to me and walked slowly to his car with Anita trailing right behind him. New York met South Carolina!

Anita happened to be the pet of the convenience store's owner and she wandered the store's property hoping to get a hand out by saying hello to folks that stopped in. She was a local celebrity and guaranteed to get a laugh from travelers that jump off the interstate to pump some gasoline and get some refreshments. For the record Anita weighed in at least 300 pounds give or take.

Free Ride

Did you know that you could make millions of dollars from the NBA for doing nothing? Back in 1976 when the National Basketball Association merged with the American Basketball Association resulting in four new teams joining the NBA. The "newbie's" were the New

York Nets, San Antonio Spurs, Denver Nuggets and the Indiana Pacers. In the agreement two solvent ABA franchises the Spirits of St. Louis and the Carolina Cougars agreed to cease operations. The folding of the two ABA teams did not come free. The owners of the Spirits, the Silna Brothers of St Louis were the beneficiaries of a negotiated lifetime share of the League's television deal that was instituted in 1976. This agreement brought them an initial payment estimated at $20 million dollars. At last check the value received for doing nothing has exceeded more than $300 million dollars. It should be pointed out that the NBA is currently in vigorous negotiations to end this thirty-eight year agreement with the Silna Brothers? In the interim, the checks keep coming.

Faux Pas

I'm reminded of a few stories by one of my former television analysts Mike Gminski. "G-Man" is a Duke graduate and a 14 year veteran of the NBA with stops in New Jersey, Philadelphia, Charlotte and Milwaukee. During college basketball season you can catch Mike as a CBS Sports Analyst covering the NCAA Men's Championship and his expertise is also seen on Fox where he covers the Atlantic Coast Conference. It was Mike who helped educate me in some of life's better things; wine, cigars and good food. Many an evening was spent in hotel and restaurant bars with Mike discussing everything from politics to religion. Mike was a solid member of the GOP and if I leaned any more left I'd fall down. Art Linkletter the famous television host of the late 1950's and early 1960's used to say, "Kids say the darn'dest things." Well guess what? Adults do too especially after a few drinks.

We were in Salt Lake City for a game against the Jazz and the night before we were looking for a place to dine. Our Producer John Guagliano was assigned the task of finding a restaurant for the night.

John at the time was young, single and Italian. At the front desk he spotted two very attractive blondes and he saddled up next to them and began a conversation by asking the ladies for a restaurant and their recommendation. They both looked at John and in unison said, "Italian right?" John's responded "Absolutely!" With that we were on our way with our "Little Italian."

There are a few city ordinances that mystified me about Salt Lake City. One is you have to "become a member" of the establishment you visit before you can order an alcoholic beverage and two, they sell near beer and they only pour from individual single serving bottles. The very same bottles are the kind you would receive flying the friendly skies. Thankfully, the city fathers have removed these restrictive blue laws with the reason given; the Winter Olympics.

This time I was the one who inadvertently put his "foot in his mouth." After dinner, we all adjourned as duly signed members to the restaurant bar for some after dinner drinks along with some very robust cigars. All was well and we're having a good old time when I noticed a younger Asian man entering the bar on crutches with a fresh cast that was up to his thigh. He hobbled over to a nearby chair and sat down and he was joined by two young Asian ladies. He appeared to be fresh from the Emergency Ward while his friends had just returned from the mountains. Without even thinking I opened my mouth and said to the Asian gentleman, "Tough day on the slopes!" For a few seconds there's absolute silence then everyone is rolling in laughter. I suddenly realized what I had said and I was totally embarrassed. I was referring to the man's accident on the mountain skiing; but instead uttered what could be construed as a racist remark. It was a classic open mouth before engaging brain moment. I apologized profusely while my party rolled in laughter at my embarrassment.

Another way we used to spend our time on the road was watching television. Once in a while we'd get together as a group for a night of viewing someone's personal movie collection. We were in Cleveland and, we scheduled a Godfather marathon. We were going to plow through Godfather I, II and III. Working with the hotel, our radio analyst Gerry Vaillancourt arranged to have a private room, television, VCR and room service all set up and ready for us. Vaillancourt a big fan of the "Wise Guy "genre is always asking "Do you remember the scene from" such and such?" We settled in for what we knew was going to be a very long evening. Only predicament; the television was not working. Not a problem! Mike Gminski our television analyst headed up to his room and he proceeded to liberate the "locked down" television from its security mount and carried it on the elevator and down to the conference room where we were encamped. Room Service arrived and we settled in watching the Trilogy. We are like kids at a Saturday Matinee mouthing the lines and having a great old time. We made it through I and II without much difficulty. We noticed Vaillancourt was fading and fading fast. We all agreed that it was all or none from start to finish in watching this marathon and now, the principal organizer was ready to throw in the towel and go off to bed. Gerry was gone! We spent the rest of our Godfather III viewing ragging on him for his desertion. For the record we finished viewing of all three movies in just about 9 hours.

One beer too many

All NBA teams play pre-season games. These contests are played in various venues around the United States. Their purpose is to:

a) Give the players some early competition away from the rigors of Training Camp,

b) Fan exposure

c) Money

Promoters around the country relish the opportunity and pay big bucks to have two NBA teams come to their town and play in their local arena. This was the case when the Celtics went to Columbus, Ohio for a pre-season game at Ohio State University. In the days before luxury charters teams always had to stay in the city or town where they played electing to leave commercially the following morning. Our hotel was not the Ritz but more of a three story motel type with rooms facing a courtyard and pool.

This story involved two players and one reporter. The culprits: Kevin McHale and Danny Ainge. The victim: Mike Carey the Beat Writer assigned to cover the Celtics for the Boston Herald. Each team traditionally has a beat writer assigned to cover every game both home and away. Like a travelling circus we're all family. After most games we would all look for a restaurant or bar where we could get a bite and relax and unwind. This night in Columbus was no different. Players and reporters always socialized and Mike was friendly with both Kevin and Danny.

You should know that both Kevin and Danny have a mischievous streak in their DNA and it sometimes rears its head in a funny way. The three, McHale, Ainge and Carey were together after the game. It became obvious Carey had too much to drink.   After a while he was helped back to his room where he could lie down and sleep it off. Here, is where the mischief if you want to call it that, began.

They assisted Mike back to his room where they put him to bed. Mike was out cold from too much alcohol and was oblivious to what was happening around him. Kevin and Danny proceeded to gather everything in the room: towels, sheets, pillow cases, even Mike's clothing. They then filled his bathtub with water and deposited all the items including what Mike was wearing into the tub. The final coup d'état, they then turned into instant artists. With use of a marker pen they proceeded to extend his sideburns and they gave him a new hairline with exaggerated eyebrows. As they departed they drew the drapes wide open, left all the lights on and exited with poor Mike passed out on the bed for the whole world to see.

Danny Ainge is the current General Manager of the Boston Celtics. In his day he was a scrappy little guard. After a few years of playing major league baseball as an infielder Danny was drafted by the Celtics in 1981. A huge part of the Celtics success in the 1980's Ainge has moved on to wearing a management hat for the successful franchise. After eight years with the Celtics Danny was traded to the Sacramento Kings in 1989 for Ed Pinckney and Joe Kleine. The interesting story behind this trade was it was executed after the Celtics had played in Sacramento on February 23rd beating the Kings 99 to 91. The Celtics were on a red-eye heading east when the trade was consummated and Danny did not know he had been traded. Landing in Chicago to change planes for the flight continuation to Boston most of the team tried to catch a bit of sleep. Tired, Danny laid down on the floor when Steve Bulpett of the Boston Herald gently covered the sleeping Ainge with his own overcoat. While Danny was sound asleep between the aisles of chairs, Celtic Team Massage Therapist, Vladimir Shulman seeing Ainge sleeping soundly got a crazy idea. You have to know that Vladimir is from the Soviet Union and he still has a thick Russian accent.

Standing in front of the sleeping Ainge, Shulman started stopping travelers passing by asking them in his heavy Russian inflection, "Is *street man, give him few bucks."* To this day we're still not sure how much money was donated to the sleeping street man but then we'll never know. Later that day he found out he was no longer a Celtic.

It takes two hands…

Tim Kempton was an original Hornet. He was left unprotected by the Los Angeles Clippers in the Expansion Draft of 1988 and was immediately taken by the Charlotte Hornets as part of their first-ever team building effort. Joining Tim on this newly formed squad were veterans Kurt Rambis and Kelly Tripucka along with First-Round pick from Kentucky, Rex Chapman. The 1988-1989 edition of the Charlotte Hornets immediately won over the hearts of the community that responded by filling the Charlotte Coliseum to capacity. For Tim what started out as an innocuous discussion with a fellow teammate eventually turned into a sharp criticism from his Head Coach Dick Harter?

Here is what started as a simple conversation between two individuals on the team bus. Kempton related,

"Since we were new, we had reporters travelling with us. Kurt Rambis asked me, what was the biggest thing I've ever eaten?

Kempton it should be noted was 6 feet 10 inches tall and weighed in at 245 pounds.

Responding to his teammate Rambis, Kempton nonchalantly acknowledged,

"I ate a "Whopper" one day in one bite."

Well Rambis dramatically reacted to Tim's comment catching the attention of the reporter that was assigned to cover the Team. Well, by the time the bus ride was over the casual conversation had turned into a full-grown challenge.

Kempton continued "Now, the reporter made a big deal out of it and he turned it into a challenge for our checks (per diem money)."

As a result of the challenge, Tim ended up at his favorite Longhorn Steak House in Charlotte where, in front of a large crowd succeeded in proving his claim of eating a burger in one bite. His devouring of the hamburger was a front-page sports story in the Charlotte Observer complete with pictures of his gastronomic accomplishment.

With all the publicity generated from his gluttonous contest one of the first to weigh in on what he had done was his Head Coach, Dick Harter. Kempton went on,

"He (Harter) didn't really take kindly that I was stuffing "Whoppers" in my mouth. He thought I should be working more on basketball and I told him, Dick come on it was for charity it was a funny, goofy thing I don't do it every day."

Kempton summed it up best, "It was fun we had a great time with it we gave $500 dollars to charity but I don't think it endeared me with Dick Harter too much."

Mugged

You're not supposed to get injured attempting to enter or leave an NBA game; especially if you're attending as a spectator. One would think you would be safe walking from your car to the arena and vice versa. The old Miami Arena was located a few blocks in from Biscayne Boulevard in a seedy run down section of town. At times it was a gauntlet of homeless people who occupied the area and they constantly harassed game attendees making their way to the arena. All available parking was in close vicinity of the building and required most patrons to walk to the venue. Local authorities tried their best to insure the safety of the fans; only sometimes stuff happens. Now, imagine if you're a celebrity attending the game and you ended up being a victim of a mugging. Back in 1990 professional golfer Jan Stephenson the winner of several LPGA Championships was the target of a miscreant bent on doing her harm. She left her car accompanied by friends to attend the Heat/Phoenix Suns game on January 23, 1990. Just before leaving the parking lot she was putting her purse in the trunk when out of nowhere a low-life swooped in and mugged her for her handbag. This occurred directly adjacent to the arena. Immediately police swarmed the area and no luck finding the perpetrator. Unfortunately for Jan the scuffle that ensued resulted in her finger being broken. The injury jeopardized her professional career for a short while as she recuperated. Eventually her career as a golfer continued and to this day, her finger still has a crook in it to remind her of what happened that evening in Miami.

Chapter 8

Coaches and Leadership

I have had the privilege to work with many coaches over the length of my career. Additionally, I have witnessed the rise of players into the coaching ranks from the teams I was associated with.

I was with some for quite a while and others for just a short time. I'd like to recognize them for being a part of my career and my personal development. They are: K. C. Jones, Jimmy Rodgers, Jim Lynam, Doug Moe, Fred Carter, Allan Bristow, Dave Cowens, Paul Silas, Tim Floyd, Byron Scott, Jeff Bower and Monty Williams.

Additionally, there are players who have become head coaches that I had the opportunity to work with and they are: Rick Carlisle, Brian Shaw, Kevin McHale and Jeff Hornacek along with numerous assistant coaches from over the years.

I've selected a few of my favorite coach stories to share with you.

Fred Carter

During the 1992-1993 Season Fred "Mad Dog" Carter was the late-season replacement as interim Head Coach of the Philadelphia 76ers after Doug Moe's departure. Carter had been toiling as a Sixers Assistant Coach on a team that was going nowhere.

Fred was a member of the famed 76er Team of 1972-1973. That Team had the notoriety of being the worst team in NBA history winning a paltry nine games for a final record of nine wins and seventy-three losses.

That Philadelphia record unfortunately still stands today.

Charles Barkley was gone. He was traded to Phoenix for a troika of veteran journey men including Jeff Hornacek, Tim Perry and Andrew Lang. Fred's team was stocked with players nearing the end of their careers as well as some un-seasoned rookies.

This mish-mash of a team was assembled by the owner; Harold Katz who decided it was a time for a change. The 76ers were going nowhere fast.

With Carter at the helm, the lowly Sixers finished off the season winning just 7 games while losing 19. For the affable Carter the 1992-1993 was one to forget. His Sixers ended up with a final record of 26 wins and 56 losses.

Throughout his time as "Interim Head Coach" Fred Carter was a preacher when it came to basketball. He drilled his player's daily to play full throttle defense and work as a team on offense.

As a coach Fred was animated when he was on the sideline. Constantly haranguing the officials Carter would be seen working them and trying to get the advantage. Additionally he was a constant source of verbal inspiration to his players as he cajoled them to play and play hard.

Toward the end of the season I was home with an infrequent night off and I was watching television waiting for sports to come on hoping I could catch some Sixers' highlights.

Half paying attention to what was on the television I noticed they had started their segment on "what happened around the NBA." I perked up when they started the Sixers' highlight package. Nothing happened on the screen that was out of the ordinary until I saw something and I said to myself, "Did I see what I just saw?"

There was no reference as to what I had thought I had witnessed. The sports segment moved on to their next story. Determined to verify what I thought I had seen I waited around to catch the re-broadcast. You have to remember this was long before there were DVR devices available. When the re-broadcast came on I scrutinized the sports package and sure enough I was not crazy. It happened during the highlight they "cut away" to a shot of Fred animated on the sideline when suddenly, he spit out his denture and without missing a beat retrieves it in mid-air and puts it back in his mouth. They always did say when Fred played he was known for his quick hands.

Rick Carlisle

Rick Carlisle, a friend and Head Coach of the Dallas Mavericks is an example of just what it takes to be a successful head coach. Carlisle, attended two colleges Maine and Virginia before being drafted by the Boston Celtics in 1984. He was nicknamed "Flipper" by his Celtics teammates. Why Flipper? Carlisle had big feet and when he put on his black sneakers they looked just like swim fins. His five year run as a player led him directly into coaching. His hard work was finally rewarded with his winning the NBA Championship in 2011 with the Dallas Mavericks.

There is a theory as to who makes a better coach, is it the superstar or is it the guy who worked hard sitting at the end of the bench? Looking at the success of ex-players turned head coaches like Michael Jordan and Ervin Johnson compared to the less visible role players; the evidence shows that Phil Jackson, KC Jones and Rick Carlisle were considered successful coaches compared to the superstars.

It was related to me by Bob Cousy, also a former head coach; he (the superstar) grasped details of the game differently. Their patience with players was less due to the fact that they sometimes found it hard to believe that players could not deliver and execute the same way they did when they played. In his opinion, the better coaches came from the eighth to twelfth men on the bench.

Why?

Simply put, they have more of an opportunity to look, listen and more important learn. Just glance around the league now and see how many of the present head coaches started and or spent most of their playing careers sitting on the bench.

Today's current crop of head coaches comprises a plethora of former players who were non-starters and are now successful coaches. The list includes ex-players: Brain Shaw, Glenn"Doc" Rivers, Monty Williams, Scott Brooks and others who are coaching and teaching at the professional level.

Rick Carlisle is a successful example of this premise; the best coaches came from off-the-bench and he has the ring to prove it.

Most coaches have diversions that help them keep their sanity over a long NBA season. San Antonio's Greg Popovich dabbles in wine. Former Celtics and present Louisville Head Coach Rick Pitino was into thoroughbred race horses.

I bet you don't know one thing that separates Rick Carlisle from his peers. Many an evening after returning to our team hotel, it was a common sight if there was a piano available in the lobby or a quiet lounge to see Rick sit down and start playing. The fact that he was self-taught and played mostly by ear is phenomenal. There was more to Rick Carlisle than coaching.

Dick Harter

In a story related to me, Dick Harter was the first Head Coach hired by the expansion Charlotte Hornets in 1988. His job was to take a roster of mostly un-protected veterans and drafted rookies and put together a team.

The Charlotte Hornets of 1988 were quickly becoming a fan favorite to the residents of the Middle Piedmont of North Carolina. Veteran players like: Tyrone "Muggsy" Bogues, Dell Curry, Kurt Rambis and Kelly Tripucka along with rookie sensation Rex Chapman immediately won over the fans and the 23,000 seat Charlotte Coliseum was sold-out and rocking every night. But, as any expansion team knows, winning was difficult.

It was no different for the fledgling Charlotte Hornets.

Harter was faced with a dilemma. His Team was very weak at the Point Guard position. The two point players on his roster were "Muggsy" Bogues and Ricky Green.

Bogues, was a five foot three inch product of Baltimore basketball factory Dunbar High School. His road to the pros came with his selection in the 1987 Draft by the Washington Bullets. Left un-protected by the Bullets one year later, Bogues was taken by the Hornets in the Expansion Draft. He quickly became the fan's favorite Hornet. On the other side of the ball was Chicago son and Michigan alumni Ricky Green, a ten year, four team veteran and former first rounder was also picked by the Hornets in the Expansion Draft.

Needless to say, the Hornets were weak at the Point Guard position. This was evident to Harter and his staff. There was another problem!

With Muggsy's growing popularity came pressure from team management to play Bogues more.

There was no argument that he knew how to play the point. Every night he gave one hundred percent on the court. Bogues' playing ability and skills were second to none. The reality to Harter and his staff was that at five foot-three, Muggsy Bogues was not tall enough to play against the bigger, stronger players.

After weeks of constant pressure, Coach Harter was called into owner George Shinn's office to discuss the matter, No coach likes it when the front office is viewed as interfering yet it is the owner's prerogative to have some input. After all, it is his money that is being spent and he has the right to get involved in personnel decisions.

Harter entered Shinn's office and casually made small talk with the Hornets owner about the team in general. Then the subject switched to the point guard issue. Shinn ever the marketer stressed to Harter the importance of keeping the fan base happy as his new franchise continued to grow and thrive in the Charlotte community.

Harter on the other hand with his competitive juices flowing wanted to win and he presented his case that there needs to be a change at the point guard position. Shinn stood firm and held to his stance that Bogues was to be the point guard.

Harter with his frustration rising and his temper in control decided to confront Shinn. George Shinn was no giant. He's of average height and Harter to make his point got up from his chair, positioned himself in front of Shinn and dropped to his knees and looked Shinn straight in the eyes and blurted out-

"George, Look at me, I am your point guard!"

"How do you expect me to win?"

Harter had made his point to no avail. Shinn would have none of it. "Muggsy" Bogues was to be the starting point guard and for a while, the face of the Charlotte franchise.

The Military

Randy Ayers Assistant Coach for the New Orleans Pelicans is considered a journeyman in his profession. Coach Ayers has spent his entire adult life working as a coach. With stops at Miami of Ohio, Ohio State University, Philadelphia 76ers, Orlando Magic, Washington Wizards and the United States Military Academy Coach Ayers has a unique prospective on the game of basketball and how it should be played. With all his sojourns in coaching, by far his most rewarding experience was his time spent as an assistant coach at the United States Military Academy at West Point.

Coach Ayers has a great appreciation for the military and what it does for our country.

His admiration for the young men and women that attended the Academy stays with him. "The young people I worked with were outstanding...Good people who would run through a brick wall for you, they were very coachable."

Coach Ayers went on to say that, "I had a great experience there and to have it as my first coaching experience probably helped me in establishing my philosophy." Talking about the atmosphere of attending an event at Michie Field or the Christl Arena at West Point Ayers went on to say, "Everybody wanted to be there...I think it's something that everyone should put on their bucket list."

Talking about the coaches that went through West Point two come to mind: Bob Knight and Mike Krzyewski. Asked if he thought the Academy was a positive breeding ground for coaches. Ayers continued, "Whenever I hear Coach Knight or Coach "K" speak they talk about the pride and honor of serving West Point and our Country." Asked if he's had contact with any of his players/cadets, "the guys that I've watched, Coach K has brought to speak to our National Team."

One of them is Bobby Brown Class of 1981. "I'm proud of him and to see what he has done in using the military as a career and it's nice to see that Coach K has brought him back and he is involved with our National Team." For the record as of this date Bobby Brown is Lieutenant General Robert Brown Commander Joint Base Lewis-McChord in Washington State. Ayers went on to suggest that more young people should consider attending one of our service academies.

"You're getting a great education. You're representing your country and most important you're developing leadership skills and how to work in a large organization-teamwork that's what West Point is all about."

While we are on the subject of the military let's recognize the members of the National Basketball Association who chose to serve their Country. Some of whom we knew had served and others we did not.

David Robinson "The Admiral," Graduated from The Naval Academy in Annapolis where in reality served as a Lieutenant Junior Grade before leaving the Navy to pursue his NBA dream.*

Senator Bill Bradley also an NBA All-Star served in the United States Air Force.*

Mike Silliman is the only West Point Graduate Class of 1966 to play in the NBA and serve in the Regular Army.*

Bill Sharman was a navy man during World War II.*

The Miami Heat's Tim James enlisted in the Army and served honorably in Iraq.*

Hall of Famer George Yardley was also in the Navy.*

Current NBA Player Bernard James was in the Air Force before becoming a professional. To all who served; a big thanks for your service to our country.*

(*Courtesy NBA League News-Brian Rzeppa)

Chapter 9

The Talent

Gil Santos

Some of the talents I've worked with were plain old crazy. Gil Santos my Celtics Play-by-Play Man was a fun loving hard working individual with a great sense of humor. Gil also was a practical joker. He spared no one. For an entire season Gil and Celtic great Cedric Maxwell had an ongoing ritual of re-enacting the characters from the movie "The Pink Panther."

Depending on the day and arena they were in, one or the other would assume the role of "Kato" in order to surprise the other.

One night Cedric was going through his pre-game ritual of stretching on the court at the Boston Garden.

Gil seeing the perfect opportunity to get one over on his friend proceeded to crawl on his stomach under the scoring table unseen by all and continued to slowly slide and utter in his faux French accent, "*Kaaaaaaato! Kaaaaaato!*"

Maxwell was looking everywhere and could not see where the voice was coming from.

Santos continued to call out and Cedric had no idea where he was.

Finally when Maxwell was distracted by his stretching routine Gil slid out from under the Scoring Table to the laughter of everyone around. This time another round of the Inspector and Kato was won by Mr. Santos.

As mentioned, the broadcasting fraternity travelled together, socialized together and laughed together! Very often with our "courtside" seats we were witness to some funny happenings that most viewers and listeners never saw.

Home and visiting broadcasters are seated at the Scorer's Table adjacent to their team's bench. While fans think this is a great position to be in to view and call a game most announcers will agree it is good only until your head coach is up and animated and he's standing right in front of you. The only view you have of the game is the coach's backside.

Long before the hydration of players became a big business, players tended to replenish fluids the old fashioned way; with water or whatever was handy. I was reminded by Gil Santos of an instance involving Number 33 Larry Bird. After a Celtics timeout and with play about to commence Larry, set to inbound, turned and spied what he needed. He reached down to where Gil was sitting and picked up Santo's cup of cola and proceeded to guzzle it down. Finished he tossed the cup back to Gil without saying a word and inbounded the ball to continue playing the game.

Most broadcasts like to incorporate what in the business is called a "walk-off." This is when win or lose a quick interview is conducted with a player or coach just as they walk off the court at the end of a game. On this particular night we were in Atlanta playing the Hawks at the old Omni and Gil Santos had to do a short interview with the Hawks' Head Coach Kevin Loughrey. As part of the interview we gave the person appearing a gift courtesy of a sponsor just for the mention of their product. As Santos was wrapping up the interview he casually thanked Kevin for appearing and told him he would be getting a brand-new set of Black and Decker Power Tools just for appearing. Whereupon Loughery said on-the-air live that "he was scared to death of all power tools and did we have something else we could give him." Some of this material you can't make up.

Dining on the road was always a treat. We had very reasonable expense accounts and as my boss always used to say, "have a good time just don't go nuts." Depending on what city we were in there were restaurants we always visited. A visit to Indianapolis always meant a stop at St Elmo's Steak House. In Sacramento it was Frankie Fats, in Chicago there was Gibson's and The Rosebud. In Los Angeles we chomped down at C & O Trattoria or Dan Tana's.

Dan's was an eclectic place in West Hollywood that was frequented by those that wanted to see celebrities and those Hollywood types that wanted to be seen. It became a regular spot for us whenever we were in Los Angeles. One night during the regular season we went there for dinner and it was the usual star gazing for us too.

While we were not celebrities, we were treated well and enjoyed our evening. Sitting near the bar, the three of us happened to notice the most striking and attractive blonde sitting there with a gentleman. Not wanting to stare we carried on our dinner conversation and every now and then our eyes would wander back to the beautiful lady sitting at the bar. With coffee and after dinner drinks at hand our discussions continued when Dan himself came over to our table to see how our evening was going and if the meal and service had been to our liking? Dan also took a moment to lean over and discreetly mentioned that he had noticed that we were admiring the young lady at the bar and we acknowledged that fact. Well, to our surprise Dan leaned closer and said, "Fellows it isn't a she it's a he" then smiled and walked away. We shook our heads and in unison we exclaimed, "Hooray for Hollywood."

Mike Crispino

Mike Crispino was another of my gifted play-by-play men. He had just joined WLVI-TV Channel 56 in Boston as their Sports Anchor and was replacing Gil Santos on the Celtics broadcasts. Gil was moving on to broadcast the New England Patriots Football games on radio.

Crispino joined Bob Cousy at the broadcast desk for Channel 56's last season of broadcasting the Celtics. The contract had expired and the rights would be moving to another entity in town.

Crispino rose to the occasion and presented his listeners a pretty respectable broadcast. His partner, Bob Cousy knew what his role as the analyst was. He picked his spots where to heap praise or when to criticize the Celtics for their excellent or poor play. Cousy could get away with the criticism-Crispino could not.

It had been said that in sports, statistics indicate but videotape indicts! On this particular night, the latter was the case. The Celtics were really playing bad and Cousy was laying into them. Not in an ad homonym way but with evidence conveniently supplied by our video tape replays. Crispino continued his play-by-play staying as neutral as possible while sticking to describing the action.

In addition to his play-by-play duties, Crispino had to go into the locker room after the game and gather video and sound for the next Channel 56 Newscast.

With his photographer in tow, Mike entered the locker room where he was met by an incensed Larry Bird. Bird started berating Mike in a voice loud enough for the entire press corps and others in the locker room to hear too.

He started in by asking Mike "I heard you didn't like the way we played tonight?"

Mike responded with "What are you talking about?" Mike was certainly aware of what Cousy had said but he had kept an impartial perspective on his presentation.

Bird continued to jump all over Crispino telling him "you don't know squat about basketball" and he and the rest of the team were not going to talk to him.

Right about now, Crispino was sweating bricks. New on the job all he could think was what he was going to say to his news director and management when asked what happened and why he didn't get any player reaction for the Ten O'clock News.

Crispino was worn down by the harangues from Mr. Bird when from a few lockers away Robert Parish in his deep, deep voice uttered for all to hear;

"Hey, relax he's just f***ing with you!"

Bird looks at the Chief, Robert Parish and gave him his trademark little smile and Mike Crispino lived to report another day.

Gil McGregor

Gil McGregor former Hornets Color Analyst probably is one of the smartest individuals that I've worked with. Gil graduated from Wake Forest University in 1971 after four seasons as their starting center. Gil has spent time as a professional in the NBA, ABA and Europe including France, Belgium and Italy.

A gifted motivational speaker, McGregor has a way of getting his message to his listeners. His message to the youth in his audience is sincere, honest and straight to the point about growing up. Gil spoke on how to avoid confrontation with each other and most important respect; especially respect for women. On numerous occasions I have seen Gil bring his audience to their feet cheering as he delivered his motivational message.

Gil too is famous around the National Basketball Association for his basketball expertise and one other item.

It would be fair to say that Gil is the King of the Pun.

In almost every broadcast you can be sure that Gil would deliver his play on words. Gil very rarely used a double-entendre but more likely would deliver a pun with humor and wit.

Here are some of Gil's more memorable puns delivered during broadcasts:

On the day Coach Reggie Theus was fired from the Sacramento Kings on our broadcast that night he uttered, "People who don't like Reggie must be *A-Theust's.*"

Referring to the speed of former Hornet Darren Collison he started calling him the *"Blur de Bee."*

One night talking about Chris Paul's play against Patty Mills, he told us that *"Chris just made a Patty Melt out of Patty Mills."*

After a horrendous shooting night he once called Jeff Malone, *"Jeff Alone"* for his poor play.

Other Gil puns uttered:

Los Angeles Clipper Danny Granger, *"Danny's the Lone Granger."*

Another classic! *"Well, when you're in a dilemma, you gotta make dilemmonade."*

He has been known to change a coach's name like, *"Scott Skiles to Scott" Scowls."*

Gerry Vaillancourt

One of the benefits of travelling with a professional team is the accommodations. The Collective Bargaining Agreement with the NBA and the NBPA or National Basketball Players Association states in their agreement "those players will have to stay at a minimum of a five star rated hotel." Exceptions are granted in the Pre-Season when teams usually play in smaller markets and the population cannot support these luxury hotels. For us folks accompanying and traveling with the team it was The Ritz Carlton and The Four Seasons as well as a few first-class boutique hotels.

Gerry Vaillancourt nick-named "The V-Man" by fans was the long-time radio analyst for the Hornets happily relayed this story that happened in the span of a three day road trip. Let's add just because you're staying in a first-class hotel, doesn't mean that everything will be first-class.

It is not uncommon for teams to check in late at night or even very early in the morning after having played a game in city A and right after that checking in to a hotel in city B. Here is a basic account of what happened to one announcer at two different hotels.

Let us start with Hotel A on day one. Normally we chartered out of our home city in the mid-afternoon arriving in our opponent's city late afternoon to early evening. For our first stop, we arrived late afternoon at Hotel A-The Canterbury in Indianapolis. The Canterbury's claim to fame was that it was the location of a certain indiscretion that lead to Mike Tyson's fall from grace and an eventual prison cell.

Most of the team quickly headed up to their rooms to settle in for some television and room service. Gerry Vaillancourt is what we call a purest. His background and knowledge of basketball is superior and his work ethic and game preparation place him in the upper echelon of his peers. Gerry doesn't check in right away. He's started his game preparation by searching out the nearest news stand to pick up the local newspapers to read up on our next opponent.

Returning to the hotel, he picked up his key, boarded the elevator to his floor and his assigned room. I'm in my room watching television when I heard someone trying to get in to my room.

I looked thru the peep-hole and there's Gerry.

I yelled, "Hey, go find your own room." He replied this is my room."

I quickly scanned the rooming list and told him that he's in Room XYZ and off he goes.

At Room XYZ he encounters another person as he tried to enter the room. From behind the door, he heard a gentleman with a thick Indian accent telling him *"go away"* and that he was going to call the police.

Sure enough within moments two hotel security guards approached Gerry wanting to know what's up. Gerry explained who he was and showed proper identification when one of the guards told him there had been a room change and they were sorry for any inconvenience it may have caused.

Under the escort of the two security people Gerry was delivered to a room that they said was his. Without pausing one of the guards opened the room door with his master key and Gerry walked into the room.

Oops, Big Mistake! Gerry and Security were greeted by a woman in the bed and a man coming out of the shower with a can I help you look on his face. Security asked, "Is this your room Sir?" Clearly disturbed the man responded, "No, I just wanted to take a shower…of course it's my room." Realizing something was amiss, the two guards once again intervened apologizing profusely to the man and his lady friend. After a radio call down to the front desk, Gerry finally makes it to his assigned room. Day One ended for Gerry V at The Canterbury. Or, so we thought!

Gerry finally entered into his assigned room anticipating climbing between the sheets for a few hours of sleep before we have to do it all over again.

He undressed and readied himself for bed and he pulled down the sheets where he discovered some small curly hairs and a set of earrings. Visibly agitated, Gerry called the front desk to complain about the situation. The staffer on duty at the front desk answered his call as Gerry vented on his discovery.

Finally, the desk person tells Gerry, "Sir, I'm sorry! We will reduce the room cost by fifty percent and as far as the earrings, "you can keep them and I won't tell." He said good night! And he hung up the phone. Day one finally had ended.

Day two was a game day and we pick up our story after playing in Indianapolis and chartering to San Antonio landing in the early morning hours. We're on the bus headed to The Marriott on the city's famed Riverwalk. We all received our keys and proceeded up to our rooms beat from playing and travelling and, also knowing we have a much-welcomed day off ahead of us before we have to play another game. It's after 2am it's off to bed for all of us until the next morning.

With a full day off before the last game of the trip we settled in at the Marriott to relax. Our friend Gerry decided to be the hermit and stay in his room and watch some television and do some game preparation at the same time. He ordered room service and relaxed for the afternoon.

There was a friendly tap on his door and the Room Service Attendant wheeled in his meal cart and set it up with the usual fanfare. Gerry signed for the service and sat down to enjoy his club sandwich, potato chips and iced tea.

"Wait a minute" Gerry said as he removed the aluminum cover," I didn't order this steak, baked potato and cheesecake, I ordered a simple sandwich." Surveying the mistake, the Bellman said sorry Sir "I made a mistake; enjoy it at our expense."

Gerry says thank you very much and sat down to enjoy his new lunch.

Tap tap at the door. It's the Bellman again. "Sir, I need to get the steak back it was for another room."

Gerry responded fork and meat in hand while chewing he snickered" Hey it's too late."

The Bellman walked out mumbling something to the effect "I have a problem!"

Gerry smiled back…"Yes, you do!"

So it was on the road for one person in our traveling party.

Another classic V-Man moment happened in Charlotte, North Carolina. For the folks who have been to the Charlotte Coliseum home of the Charlotte Hornets you're aware there's only two ways to gain access to the Coliseum. One entrance is via Tyvola Street and the other rear entrance accessible by using Billy Graham Parkway/Woodlawn Boulevard. Traffic around game time for years had been the source of many bottlenecks as both fans were attempting to get to the game and commuters were heading home after work.

Gerry in addition to his Hornets duties had his daily sports talk program originating at the studios of WBT Radio. Located a short five miles and a brief fifteen minute ride from the Coliseum the V-Man had plenty of time to make the trek from WBT to the arena. This applied only when there are no major traffic issues. On this particular night it was bumper to bumper for the afternoon commute. Sitting in the stall and crawl traffic the impatient and soon to-be-late Vaillancourt decided to create his own lane of traffic. Busting out of his lane, he proceeded down Billy Graham Parkway running the breakdown lane. You guessed it! Blue lights appeared in his rear window. V Man was stopped dead by the police. He rolled down his window to greet the North Carolina State Trooper who pulled him over and started to see if he could to talk his way out of trouble.

Lucky for him, he was recognized by the trooper who happened to be a listener and said, "V is that you?"

Gerry responded "Yes, and if I don't get to the Coliseum I'm going to miss my scheduled on-air time." The trooper told Gerry, ""Give me your keys and come with me." Gerry obliged and was put in the back seat of the trooper's Crown Victoria. Vaillancourt has no idea what was going to happen next; other than a possible trip to jail for his reckless driving. Another trooper responded to the scene with his blue lights flashing and he met up with the first trooper to discuss what was going on?

The first state trooper jumped into his vehicle with "V" in the back seat and with blue light blazing and siren wailing he takes off in the direction of the Coliseum where he drops the V Man off at the back entrance and tells Gerry "do not worry about your car."

Vaillancourt ran into the arena and sat down at his position at the scorer's table just as the Hornets broadcast went on-the-air. Midway through the second quarter, Vaillancourt felt a tap on his shoulder. It's the second trooper and he handed Gerry his keys and told him, "Your car is out back in the parking lot."

Let's just say its luck when you and your voice were recognized and you're a familiar member of the media as was the case this particular evening for Gerry Vaillancourt.

Steve Martin

Another one of my play-by-play men was Steve Martin. Not "the Wild and Crazy Guy" Steve Martin but the Bangor, Maine born Steve Martin has been in broadcasting just about as long as I have. Multi-talented, Martin was the voice of the Charlotte/New Orleans Hornets as well as the Director of Broadcasting. Currently Steve is in Charlotte where he is the television voice of the Charlotte Bobcats soon to be renamed The Charlotte Hornets. It was Martin who was responsible for my moving to Charlotte in 1993 to collaborate with him on the Hornets television broadcasts for which I'm forever grateful. In addition to his NBA work, Steve's versatility is evident with his radio work as well as, his television work doing ACC Football.

But let me tell you, he's also the most accident prone announcer I have ever worked with. Every Saturday in the fall, Martin can be found doing his duty diligently describing the action on some nearby ACC Football Field. Whether it was Duke, North Carolina or Wake Forest Martin's distinctive play-by-play call could be heard throughout the Piedmont region.

So how was Martin so accident prone? On Mondays Martin would return to his office at the Hornets Training Facility in Fort Mill, South Carolina with a bandage on his head. How did Steve receive the wound?

The injury was never received before his broadcast. On most occasions if you saw Steve on television he looked spiffy for his on-camera appearances. It was after the game had ended that Steve Martin met his match. In his haste to drop off his rental car and make it to the airport terminal in time to catch that last flight home to Charlotte. Steve would unceremoniously remove his carry-on bag from the car and then slam down the trunk lid.

Only he would forget to move his head out of the way fast enough. His head met the closing trunk lid resulting in a gaping head wound that was bleeding profusely.

Instead of enjoying the short flight home with the cocktail of his choice Steve spent the flight under the concerned and watch-full eye of the flight crew with an ice compress on his head to relieve the pain. On Monday morning we'd see each other and I would look at him and say, "Trunk win the argument again?" He'd laugh and say "it sure did!" By the time for our next game the swelling had gone down and the bleeding had stopped and to the viewers watching all they could see was a small bandage on the top of Steve's bald head.

Jack Ramsay

It was a privilege for me to have had the opportunity to work with the late Dr. Jack Ramsay for two short seasons when I was travelling with the Philadelphia 76ers in the early 1990's as their television producer and director. Jack would fill-in whenever Philadelphia's regular analyst Steve Mix was not available. Jack was a Philadelphia native and a graduate of St Joseph's College. Additionally, he earned his "Doctor" status from the University of Pennsylvania.

Jack was an educator, coach and broadcaster and he combined all three disciplines to become one of the most respected individuals associated with the NBA. Both a college and pro coach, Ramsay reached the pinnacle of success by steering Bill Walton and hard hitting Maurice Lucas and the Portland Trailblazers to win the World Championship in 1977.

Doctor Jack as he was called by all his friends and acquaintances moved from the coaching ranks into the broadcasting scene. He was an expert at explaining the why's and how's of the game. His knowledge served as comfort food to the basketball hungry listeners. Whether Jack was on television or radio his impact and knowledge of the game made the subject of X's and O's understandable for everyone.

Sitting with Jack was more than a treat; it was an honor. Jack was a swimmer. It was a common site to see Jack swimming early-morning laps in the hotel pool. We are talking serious swimming. He would swim flat out for thirty minutes changing strokes on a regular basis. Jack was swimming well into his middle to late seventies. Curious over breakfast one morning I asked where he inherited his love for the water. It came from his time in the Navy.

Jack Ramsay and I had a common bond, we were both Veterans. He served during World War II and I served during the Vietnam era. Like others of what is referred to as "The Greatest Generation," Jack wanted to join the service. As a youngster of 17 he enlisted in the Navy. Jack went on to become an officer and a qualified diver and Underwater Demolition Expert aka "Frogman." He was forerunner of what is now a Navy Seal. It was in the Navy where Jack learned the tools of leadership.

Bob Licht

Most talent expects the unexpected especially when you're either on the road or at home doing a game. This was the case for Bob Licht Play by Play man for the New Orleans Hornets. Bob was a creature of habit when it comes to doing his job. You can never be prepared enough. On this particular game day in Milwaukee on March 13, 2009 it was no different for Bob except for one thing; it was his birthday. On his mind was the fact that sometimes his colleagues would take the time to recognize this milestone but Bob had no early indication of anything planned.

First stop for Bob that day was in the hotel's health club on a treadmill for a little cardio to get the blood moving. Then after an obligatory cup of coffee and newspapers he made the trip with the team to shoot-around at the Bradley Center. He checked in with the team's PR people to see if there was anything new he needed to know. From there he took his seat for the short practice.

After sitting in on the team's walk thru Bob sat down with Hornets Assistant Coach Ken Gattison where they reviewed the team's strategy for their opponent the Milwaukee Bucks. After his short face-to-face with the coach, he returned to his hotel for lunch and prepared his depth charts and go over his notes for the game. After a brief conference call with his television producer Scott Snyder, his director Gary Kirby and his broadcast partner Gil McGregor to discuss graphics and highlights for the broadcast it was nap time.

Bob would always be on the first bus to leave the hotel for the venue. There was something to his pre-game early arrival; it allowed him to get situated at the broadcast position and a chance to observe both teams as they loosened up. It was the time when both team's announcers would get together to compare notes.

The tip-off happened without a hitch as both teams played a close game with the Hornets winning 95 to 86. Bob's duties' did not stop with the game's end. As part of the televised post-game show Bob would be live in the locker room to interview players. Bob was moving between lockers when he sat down facing Hornets Forward David West. West could be counted on for his frank, honest answers to Bob's questions. When he received his cue to start from the television truck Bob began his "Q & A" with West. The interview was moving along when the viewer could see David's eyes growing large as a forewarning of what was about to happen. Bob continued his interview oblivious to what was about to take place. On live television viewers were treated to Head Coach Byron Scott "pie'ing" Bob Licht and wishing him a happy birthday. Bob was startled briefly but being the pro he was he asked David one more question with shaving cream all over his face before he tossed it to a commercial break. The locker room exploded with laughter and Bob Licht found out what his birthday gift ended up being.

Joel Meyers

This man has been blessed by the broadcasting gods for having one of the best set of pipes in the industry. His strong voice is recognized by many the moment he's heard on the sir. Joel hails from St Louis, Missouri a fertile breeding ground for sports announcers. Talent like Jack Buck, Joe Garagiola , Bob Starr and many others have honed their skills calling the games of the Cardinals, Blues or Rams. Joel has delivered the call for baseball, football, basketball and soccer. He has called the games of the Hornets/Pelicans, Los Angeles Lakers, Los Angeles Clippers and San Antonio Spurs. On the football side his voice has been heard doing the Houston Texans of the NFL, Big 12 Football, and baseball's St Louis Cardinals. He has one of the industry's most versatile voices. His love of basketball translates to his broadcasts. He does his homework for every game and has been known to go home after a broadcast to continue researching by watching the late games of future opponents.

Joel also has a strong knowledge of the vintner world. To say he's a wine connoisseur would be an understatement. This man really knows about wine! While his wine knowledge is superior; his expertise is Jazz. Joel has one of the largest private collections of recorded jazz artists. His collected works are in excess of 10,000 tracks and includes many unknown artists as well as big-name performers and musicians. He's always asking what kind of music you like. In New Orleans Joel is like a "kid in a candy store." On off nights he has frequented many of the jazz joints on Frenchman Street. In "The Big Easy" the locals leave Bourbon Street to the tourists and they congregate in the clubs on Frenchman Street like: Snug Harbor, Blue Nile and Checkpoint Charlie's. Joel and his wife Carol can be seen *La Buena Vida* enjoying the good life patronizing many of the 1,403 quality restaurants in New Orleans.

Philly connection

My two seasons with the Philadelphia 76ers was short lived but very rewarding. I had the opportunity to work with some excellent talent. On the play-by-play side Marc Zumoff, Andy Musser, Neil Funk, Greg Gumbel and Tom Mees shared their microphones with Steve Mix and Jack Ramsay. Each in their own way helped me to understand the game and its nuances. Marc Zumoff was close to a rookie when we started working together in 1991. He was involved with the Sixers as a reporter and studio host before moving into the play-by-play seat. Marc was already on his road to success as a play-by-play man when our paths crossed. His thirty plus years broadcasting the Sixers has established him as one of the premier basketball voices in America. In addition to his work as an announcer Marc is passing it on to the next generation by offering advice and coaching on how to succeed in sports broadcasting.

The late Andy Musser was the voice of the Philadelphia Phillies for close to twenty-five seasons. I had the opportunity to have him as talent for a few of my Philadelphia road games. Andy was a gentleman and helped me out greatly when I first started doing the Sixers. What people didn't know about Andy was his knowledge about brewing. I'm not talking tea. Musser was into beer. He was a connoisseur! I remembered one trip to Phoenix where we went out of our way to find this small brew-pub that Andy had heard of. We enjoyed a meal together and Andy got the lowdown on the microbrewery. He was a true gentlemen and he will be missed.

Greg Gumbel and I worked together for a few 76ers telecasts back in the early nineties. Gumbel was born in New Orleans and later moved to Chicago with his family. The ever-versatile Gumbel has done play-by-play for just about every major professional and collegiate sport. He was the first African-American to do play-by-play for a nationally televised sporting event when he worked Super Bowl XXXV in January of 2001 live from Raymond James Stadium in Tampa, Florida. The Baltimore Ravens defeated the New York Giants 34-7 on CBS.

What I remember most of my working with Greg was first and foremost his professionalism. Even though he was a "network guy, "he was courteous and well prepared even when I kept calling him Bryant during our pre-production meetings. Another interesting side to Greg was his spot-on imitation of recording star Chubby Checker.

Two other gentlemen that I was privileged to work with during my short time with the 76ers was Neil Funk and Tom Mees. Neil now resides in Chicago with the Bulls. Before Chicago he spent time doing radio in Philadelphia before moving over to the television side in 1991. Neil and his classic trademark "Ka-Boom" stayed in Philadelphia for seventeen years before moving on to the windy city of Chicago.

Tom Mees came to the 76ers for a brief fill-in capacity in the early 90's. He made the play-by-play transition from his strong sport of hockey to basketball without a hitch. For the younger generation he was one of the founding fathers at ESPN. Mees along with Bob Ley and Chris Berman were the only broadcasters from the day ESPN signed on-the-air September of 1979. The Entertainment and Sports Programming Network has been a fixture in the sports broadcasting culture. Sadly, Tom was not around to enjoy the success that followed his un-fortunate drowning in a swimming pool in 1996.

There was one common link between all the Philadelphia play-by-play announcers that I worked with and that was Steve Mix. Steve was the analyst for all the before mentioned announcers. Steve's career in the NBA lasted for thirteen seasons with stops in Detroit, Philadelphia, Milwaukee and the Los Angeles Lakers. Steve was honored with one all-star appearance during his playing career. Steve's personality and game knowledge helped him become a first-rate analyst. His experiences in basketball translated to his role in television. Hey, how many people can be cut by a team that only won nine games in a regular season and was still able to talk about it? His sense of humor was always present when Steve slapped on the headsets to do a game. Steve was also a man of principle when he decided to put his family ahead of his broadcast career. He thought it was more important to be around his family back in Ohio rather than living in a small apartment in Philadelphia for six months out of the year. Oh, another known fact about Steve; he always had a doctor for a roommate when he played for the 76ers. That doctor of course was Julius Erving.

Chapter 10

The Owners

Alan Cohen, Don Gaston and Paul Dupee

During my association with the Celtics in the 1980's the franchise was owned by the trio of Alan Cohen, Don Gaston and Paul Dupee. The team was under their direction and ownership up until 1993. During their tenure the Celtics won two championships 1984 and 1986. The threesome bought the Celtics from Harry Mangurian Jr. in September of 1983 for an estimated $15 million dollars. Don's son Paul Gaston acquired the team in 1993 and sold the team in 2002 to The Boston Basketball Partners LLC for approximately $360 million dollars.

The owners Cohen, Gaston and Dupee were unique in their understanding of what it took to run a business especially one so endeared to the community as the Celtics. The trio could best be described as smart, savvy businessmen with a unique perspective on what needed to be done to be successful. Just look at the two championships that were won under their tutelage in 1984 and 1986. The owners came to the Celtics with backgrounds in sports and entertainment and they transferred their knowledge into success.

As Mr. Cohen strongly stressed to his employees, "We are keepers of a public trust." The Celtics at the time was being managed by Team President "Red" Auerbach and General Manager Jan Volk. Basketball was Red's domain and business was in the capable hands of Volk. According to Volk the owners streamlined the decision process. Cohen said to Volk, "I want to make this crystal clear. One owner could approve a request." Even though the partners percentage of ownership may have been different Volk stressed, "we had three owners that ran the Celtics as an equal partnership." They were strong believers in empathy; especially to their employees and their customers.

Anything dealing with broadcasting was handled by Jan. I can remember many occasions when Jan and I would discuss our game coverage on television. Jan was more of a conservative in what he liked to see. He preferred to watch a game with minimal cutting or interruption. He would tell me, "Stay on the game camera more." Meanwhile I was the "young Turk" that liked to push the limits by showing viewers a little bit more.

Side tracking a bit, for the average local telecast the director usually has a minimum of five cameras at his disposal to cover a game. They are: game camera, tight camera, left and right hand-held cameras and a low slash camera. The game camera is used wide to cover the action. The tight camera is the tight shot camera. The hand-held cameras are traditionally placed under each basket to be used to shoot free throws and court-level replays. And, the low slash camera is placed diagonal to a team's bench to provide a different angle and perspective. Getting back to the Celtics ownership.

There were high points and low points under the trio's ownership; two world championships for the people of Boston in 1984 and 1986. Sadly there were some devastating events that rocked the franchise to its foundation. Tragedy struck the day after the NBA Draft on June 17, 1986. When people woke up on June 19th they were greeted by the news that the Celtics First Round Pick Len Bias had collapsed and died on the University of Maryland Campus. Many in Boston speculated that Len was drafted by the Celtics to assist in prolonging Larry Bird's career. Misfortune struck the Celtics again with the death of Reggie Lewis on July 27, 1993. He died while participating in an off-season pick-up game. Reggie was poised on the steps for the next level of basketball stardom; steps he never climbed.

George Shinn

George Shinn the first owner of the Charlotte Hornets was quite a guy. George was a self-made man who was able to parlay a janitor's salary and turn it into a small fortune.

George would always tell us how in high school he graduated last in his class at Kannapolis High School in North Carolina where his mother encouraged him not to feel bad. She said, "Just think of yourself as the anchor that held everybody else up."

It was George Shinn whom David Stern called on a glorious Carolina spring day in 1987 to tell him that he had been awarded a coveted NBA expansion franchise. For a while all was well in Charlotte for George and his Hornets.

When the business community and climate in Charlotte soured on Shinn because of his desire to build a new arena for his Hornets, the old money of Charlotte did its best to squeeze George simply because he was not in their club. George was a tough businessman who liked to be told the truth. In my opinion, George was forced by the NBA to take on a minority partner who poisoned the well in Charlotte ultimately forcing the Hornets to move to New Orleans. In a strange event even to this day, The City of Charlotte rejected Shinn's offer to help pay for a new arena in downtown Charlotte forcing Shinn's hand. The city and citizens of Charlotte lost the Hornets to New Orleans. Truth be told, the city of Charlotte and its new NBA franchise-The Bobcats ended up costing Charlotte millions more then it would have cost them if they had agreed to build the very same arena for the Hornets. While the arena issue swirled around, George was charged with sexual assault on a woman by the State of South Carolina; George was forced to fight for his innocence.

Here's where this story gets interesting for me. I remember the day like it just happened yesterday. At around 5:30 am on September 6, 1997 I received a call from Steve Martin the Hornets play-by-play man and the team's Director of Broadcasting to meet up with my co-worker John Guagliano and head down to Mr. Shinn's Tega Cay, South Carolina lake house. We were directed to check in with the South Carolina State Trooper on duty and he would let us in to the house where we were instructed to video tape and document the damage done by investigators during their pre-dawn entry.

John and I arrived at the house and immediately we were greeted by a gaggle of local North and South Carolina television and radio stations all eager to find out what we were doing there. We checked in with the trooper who verified our identification and he let us through the gate. Once inside, we begin the process of documenting the damage. The entire house had been dusted for finger prints. Sections of carpet were cut and removed and even the commodes and vanities were tested. Finishing the job, we packed our gear and walked out the door to head back to our office. We were greeted by the attending members of the press who were shooting video and asking, "What were you doing in there?" We respectfully declined comment and left the scene. Later we were to find out that the lead story on every television station had video and audio of "Hornets Officials"(John and I) seen leaving the Tega Cay home of George Shinn and they declined comment. His attorney Charlotte lawyer Bill Diehl represented George in a short nationally televised trial that eventually ruled that George Shinn was not guilty of sexual assault.

Working for George Shinn was a unique experience. He was extremely loyal to those who worked for him. In fact, a couple of little known facts about George was when the NBA had its first-ever player lockout most other team's laid-off staff. Not George he stood behind his people and no one ever missed a paycheck.

A more telling picture of George Shinn's generosity was after Hurricane Katrina laid waste to New Orleans and the Gulf Coast. The Hornets had nowhere to play. With a large majority of its population displaced all around the United States, New Orleans could not support a professional basketball team as it struggled to recover.

Forced out by nature, the staff of the Hornets set up temporary offices in Houston courtesy of the Houston Rockets. We learned that Oklahoma City had presented the league with a sweetheart deal to get the Hornets to play temporarily at Oklahoma City's spanking new Ford Center. We had two weeks to move the entire franchise. With staff scattered all around the United States; orders came to report to Oklahoma City.

There were casualties. Forced by familiar reasons or a desire to stay in New Orleans, some people opted not to join the team in Oklahoma City. For those of us who did, it turned into a wonderful experience for two seasons before the Hornets returned to New Orleans.

Back to George and his loyalty. It was not public knowledge but George made sure that his employees who were paying mortgages in Louisiana were not forced to pay another while living temporarily in Oklahoma City. In fact, George Shinn generously paid for my family's four-bedroom apartment in Norman, Oklahoma for two seasons.

Working for George was a pleasure.

Harold Katz

Another interesting owner was a former dentist turned sports entrepreneur, Harold Katz. Katz is often referred to as the one man that allegedly destroyed the Philadelphia 76ers during his tenure. Why do I say this? Simply looking back at the 1986 Draft and you'll understand why. The 76ers passed on Michael Jordan and made a series of trades that were regarded as one the poorer trades in the league's history. First they traded icon Moses Malone to Washington for Jeff Ruland. The end result of the trade was Moses saw the Promised Land and Ruland drowned after the sea closed in. To add insult Katz also oversaw the trading of their number one draft pick to the Cleveland Cavaliers for an obscure veteran Roy Hinson and cash considerations. That number one pick turned out to be Brad Daugherty. It was time to pound the nails into their coffin-the 76ers were dead then and for the immediate future. Let's also not forget the deal that also sent Charles Barkley to the Phoenix Suns.

Katz was a classic owner/meddler. He would not let the people he hired do their jobs. His blunders continued. In the 1989 draft Katz instructed his minions to use their 19th pick to take Kenny Payne from the University of Louisville. When asked why he picked Payne his response said something to the effect," he shot well at my backyard court." Payne went on to play four seasons averaging a paltry three points and one rebound per game.

In 1996 Harold Katz eventually sold his Philadelphia 76ers to Comcast-Spectacor for an estimated 130 million dollars. Not a bad payoff for Katz who originally shelled out 12 million dollars to buy the 76ers in 1981.

Tom Benson

Tom Benson my newest boss and current owner is a unique individual. At eighty-six years of age he still plays an active part in the day-to-day operations of not one but two professional franchises; The New Orleans Saints and The New Orleans Pelicans.

Tom is a very hands on businessman. It is not uncommon to see him early in the morning and very late in the afternoon walking around the office greeting staff and checking on our welfare and what we're working on.

In the short time that Tom Benson has owned the team, he has fast-tracked many improvements that have shown his commitment to winning and encouraging the continued growth to both the Saints and the Pelicans.

First a little background on how he acquired the Hornets.

In December of 2010 George Shinn and his minority Partner Gary Chouest agreed to sell their interest in The New Orleans Hornets to the National Basketball Association for around 300 million dollars. The team was then owned and operated by the NBA.

Fresh off their Super Bowl XLIV win in 2010, Tom Benson began to quietly inquire into the Hornets availability? As understood by insiders he backed off, not sure he wanted to be the owner of two professional franchises in the same city.

Commissioner David Stern asked Jack Sperling an executive with the Minnesota Wild Hockey Team to oversee the Hornets operations and more important, improve profitability and screen for potential buyers. Rumors abound with names of a myriad of potentials investors like: Yahoo Co-Founder, David Filo and swim suit maker Raj Bhathal both of whom expressed an interest in purchasing the franchise. With prodding from his wife Gayle, Tom Benson began to quietly inquire again into the Hornets availability. Prompted by the rumors of a potential sale and more important a possible move out of New Orleans, Tom Benson again was in the hunt.

With the sale of the Hornets imminent and the league about to announce the purchase, it was revealed that the Commissioner gave Mr. Benson one last call and asked if would like to put a bid in for the franchise? With Gayle at his side he told Commissioner Stern, Yes, he was indeed interested in buying the team.

On April 13, 2012 the banner on the *New Orleans Times-Picayune Newspaper* read, "Tom Benson buys the New Orleans Hornets from the NBA."

The Tom Benson era had begun. As mentioned earlier, Mr. Benson's presence and commitment was visible almost immediately,

First and foremost, he calmed a very nervous Hornets Staff that everyone was safe as he began operation of the team.

Second, he immediately began work on securing and building a first-class training facility on the grounds of his existing Saints facility on Airline Drive in Metairie. Tom and his senior management team of Dennis Lauscha and Mickey Loomis agreed that in order to attract quality free-agents they needed a first-class training facility. Well that new facility was built and is up and running. In fact, the Saints and Pelicans are probably the only professional teams that practice on the same campus.

Thirdly, the inevitable had to happen. The Hornets was the team's original name going back to its Charlotte days. Tom Benson wanted the name changed to a more Louisiana type handle that could be identifiable with the entire gulf coast region. So, that desire gave birth to the New Orleans Pelicans.

Ironically, the Hornets name was returned to Charlotte where they will be dropping the present name of Bobcats and return as the Hornets for the start of the 2014-2015 Season.

Oh, on a final note about Mr. Benson. How many companies do you know that provides his employees lunch every day? Football players, basketball players, coaches and staff all share a common dining room for lunch. We are not talking "fast" food; we are served restaurant quality hot meals as well as a plethora of nutritional items daily from soups, sandwiches and salads.

David Stern

I would be amiss if I were to leave off David Stern as an owner. On December 6, 2010, the league officially bought out Majority Owner George Shinn and Minority Owner Gary Chouest to take over the operation of the New Orleans Hornets. The NBA spent in excess of 300 million dollars to gain control of the struggling franchise. The league set the wheels in motion to find a new owner and at the same time made sure the team was profitable and viable for purchase. This was all accomplished when New Orleans Businessman, Tom Benson agreed to purchase the Hornets in a deal that was finalized and announced on April 13, 2012.

Stern retired as the Commissioner in February of 2014 and was the longest-tenured Commissioner in NBA history. Stern was at the helm for 30 years starting in 1984. David Stern was employed by the owners to act on their behalf and to operate their league with honesty and integrity. Some have even said his main job was to protect the owners from their biggest obstacle-the owners themselves.

Commissioner Stern made his final visit to New Orleans on November 8, 2013 to reflect on his 30 years at the helm of the NBA. Highlights of his tenure included: a lucrative television agreement with ABC, ESPN and Turner Broadcasting. Expansion to include seven cities: The new kids were Charlotte, (twice), Miami, Memphis, Sacramento, Minnesota, Toronto and Vancouver.

It was incredible that the 2014 All Star Game was seen in over 200 territories and countries. And the world tuned in to watch the best athletes on the planet as they competed in New Orleans for All Star 2014. It proved to be just what David Stern had envisioned; a global NBA. He brought labor peace with a Collective Bargaining Agreement with the players at the price of four player lockouts. In addition, a lucrative revenue sharing partnership with the teams as a result of strong merchandise sales.

One lowlight of his time in office, relocation! Stability for all franchises has always been a goal for the NBA. Team relocations which included the Hornets from Charlotte to New Orleans and the Seattle Supersonics to Oklahoma City, the Kings from Kansas City to Sacramento, the Clippers from Buffalo to San Diego /Los Angeles, the Nets from New Jersey to Brooklyn and the Grizzlies from Vancouver to Memphis all were viewed as disrupting the stability of the league. Personally, I found the Commissioner to be a very approachable, witty individual who was not afraid to tell you what he thought. After all these years, it made me feel good that whenever I would see him he would always greet me personally by my name.

Every year prior to the start of each NBA Season, all the broadcasters gathered for their annual league meetings. Traditionally, held in New York or New Jersey these meetings gave the broadcasters in attendance the opportunity to go over any new rules, view other team's "best practices," attend breakout sessions to discuss improving our product as well as, the Commissioner's "State of the League" presentation.

One particular morning during a pause between sessions my Executive Director Josh Richardson and I headed for the break area to refresh our coffee cups when I noticed the Commissioner standing in front of me pouring a cup of coffee. Without hesitation I said, "Good Morning Kiddo," (I call everybody Kiddo) and without even turning around he responded, "Mr. Shuman, how are you? I figured I'd run into you today." My Executive Director Josh Richardson to this day still likes to tell the story that "You wouldn't believe it but Shuman called the Commissioner Kiddo."

Another time where I gained even more respect for the Commissioner was again at the League's Broadcast Meetings. The Hornets has just been displaced by Hurricane Katrina in 2005 and the team had just relocated to Oklahoma City to play temporarily at the Ford Center while the City of New Orleans began its recovery from Katrina. With over 80 per cent of the city under water and devastated by the eventual loss of at least 1,800 souls, rumors swirled all around about the team, New Orleans, Oklahoma City and our futures.

I approached Maureen Coyle of the NBA Public Relations Office with a request. Bob Licht the Hornets Television Play by-Play Voice, Sean Kelley the Hornets Radio Voice and I wondered if we could have a brief moment with the Commissioner to discuss what was on our minds? We went back to our meetings. Later in the day Maureen signals to us to come over. We were ushered into an office followed by the Commissioner and his Assistant Commissioner Adam Silver.

David Stern and Adam Silver gave us all the time we wanted to ask whatever we desired about the "State" of the Hornets and its viability as a franchise and potential new ownership. Commissioner Stern was candid and direct and answered every question we had. Out of respect for the courtesy and time he extended to us I will not reveal what was said in that room that day. But I will disclose that on August 13, 2012 seven years after meeting with him in that New Jersey conference room, David Stern walked up to me just prior to the start of the Press Conference announcing Tom Benson's purchase of the Hornets and said, " Lew, I told you it would all work out." And, he was right!

Chapter 11

Toot the Whistle

Relax

NBA referees are the most underrated, misunderstood people in professional sports. Their role is to keep order, officiate fairly and most important protect the integrity of the game. They are the brunt of abuse from players, coaches as well as, the fans who verbally assault them on every occasion.

What is not known by the general public is that the officials in the NBA are the most scrutinized and trained officials in all of the major sports leagues.   Their job has no room for error; the stakes are too high. This is not to say they get it right every time but chances are upon review of the play in question it usually ends with the official being spot on accurate.

Constantly under review by the league office, the officials are held accountable for their performance. Games are monitored at NBA headquarters in New York as well as on-site observers in every venue who chart every play, foul and disputed call. Now, if there is uncertainty about a particular foul, three-point shot or out-of-bounds play, the officials have the ability to communicate with the television mobile units that are broadcasting the game and request a replay for review.

Located at the scorer's table is a device called the Referee Replay Box? The replay box is connected to the television truck broadcasting the game. This tool allows the officials (three per game) to request a replay of a disputed play from the game taking place. On most nights they have two options; the home broadcast or the away telecast. One other note, they have a two-minute time limit in which to review the various replay angles before they have to make their final decision.

The League has established various criteria in which video replay are used.

For the 2013-2014 Season the League has established fourteen Points that qualify for review. Examples of reviewable items include:

Made basket at end of period*

Foul at end of period*

Flagrant Fouls*

Player altercation*

Clock malfunction*

Two-point or Three point Field Goal*

Shot Clock Violation on made field goal attempt or foul*

Out of Bounds*

Clear Path Foul*

Correct Free Throw Shooter*

24 second reset*

Restricted Area (illegal contact question)*.

(*Courtesy: NBA Rule Book P49 Section 1)

In addition to replays you need to know that all officials in the NBA are regularly schooled in their trade by the league. This schooling is a constant learning cycle that the referees are put through. Once a year, the officials assemble for camp. It is at referee camp where they get the opportunity to go over new rules, reinforce old rules and work on officiating technique by watching, reviewing and critiquing previously officiated games. These camps usually coincide with the League Broadcast Meetings and the broadcasters are given the opportunity to sit with the officials to get a taste of how they function.

This meeting with broadcasters can bring out some feisty arguments on whether the correct call was made in a certain game. In fact, the officials relish the part of the meeting where the roles are reversed as the broadcasters become the official. Under the leadership of Joe Borgia and his fellow league officials they hand out a questionnaire with a dozen or so scenarios which are supported by video in a "you make the call," format. Numerous broadcasters are picked to pass judgment on whether the call was correct and why? A fair number get it right while a few get it totally wrong. After friendly chiding and laughter we realized just what this exercise accomplished; it provided the broadcasters a proper perspective on just how hard the job of officiating can be.

There are currently sixty-two active fulltime referees in the NBA working in three person crews. They include veteran officials as well as rookies and yes, there is a woman official Violet Palmer along with several other ladies in the system working to make it as officials in the NBA. With these sixty-two officials you get to see all kinds of personalities. Some officials have earned the knick-name "rabbit-ears" because they hear everything and tend to in our humble opinion to blow the whistle a little more than most. Others lean toward the dramatic with accentuated gestures when making a call. Most are conscientious people with great personalities.

In the heat of basketball battle tensions often run high. Players are pushing the limits. Coaches are getting into the faces of the officials and the fans are not helping by booing and haranguing the officials at every opportunity. While all this is happening the officials are trying to keep order and most important; control of the game. Every now and then we hear of an official reacting in a way that deserves of re-telling.

Remember, the officials have the use of replay to resolve certain calls that may come in dispute. The official simply puts on the headset at the Scorer's Table pushes his talk button and requests to look at the play in question. Here is a story that was related to us at our league meetings.

One night, Veteran NBA Official Bennett Salvatore was presiding over a game at the Prudential Center in Newark. The Prudential Center was serving as the temporary home for the New Jersey Nets prior to their move to Brooklyn and their new home in the brand-new Barclays Center. Tensions were high and it appeared that Bennett was in a no nonsense mood. Late in the game with a questionable call that required review, Salvatore donned the headset to talk to Nets Producer Frank DiGraci.

Now Frank like most producers in television sports names their playback devices with either names or letter. In his case his EVS or Electronic Video Server is labeled with letters X, Y and Z. Frank cordially greeted Bennett,

"What would you like to see?"

Bennett proceeded to tell the truck just what play he wanted to see.

Frank issued the command to his tape room, "Roll X."

Salvatore immediately started yelling into the headset, "Don't tell me to relax!" and he repeats it again, "Don't tell me to relax just show me the play. "

The television truck gave Salvatore the play he was looking for and confirmed the correct call was made and everyone was happy.

You can guess what came up at the following season's broadcast meetings and the referees understood the difference between roll X and relax.

T 'em Up!

The date was November 7, 2002 and the Los Angeles Lakers were in New Orleans to play the Hornets in their first year of operation in the Crescent City. This was game six for the Hornets 2002-2003 Season. The Hornets had relocated to New Orleans after a disastrous dance with Charlotte City Fathers for a new arena that went south and eventually forced the Hornets to move from the Queen City to the Crescent City.

The Hornets were off to a quick 5-0 start when the very talent laden Lakers arrived for their first regular season appearance in New Orleans. Kobe Bryant, Shaquille O'Neal and associates were sporting their own 5-1 start for a game that had all the excitement of an early playoff game.

Assigned to work the match was three journeymen officials: Joe DeRosa, Monty McCutchen and Scott Wall. All three were known for their fairness and a "no bull" attitude toward the players and coaches.

Let's move to the Second Quarter in a very physical game when out of the blue Scott Wall at the 8:22 mark suddenly blows his whistle. He signals a technical foul in the direction of the Hornets bench. Everyone was wondering what was going on? Then, he approached the Scorer's

Table and after consultation, security was called over. Scott Wall had called a Technical Foul on the home team because a fan had thrown something at him and he was requesting security remove the guilty party. To the amazement of all present, the security people escorted the "object-thrower" from the arena.

Two beefy, yellow-jacketed New Orleans Arena Security Officers proceeded to direct 85 year old Grandmother and Hornets Fan Marion Bright out of her seat and out of the arena. It seems Marion, who sits courtside was frustrated with the call made by the official and in protest threw a peanut in Wall's direction. This official's action was probably the only eviction ever of an 85 year old silver-haired grandmother from an NBA arena for tossing a peanut.

Worry not for Marion. Team Officials seeing what had transpired immediately came to Marion's rescue. First, the people who have courtside seats or as the team's refer to them as "Feet on the Floor "pay a lot of money for this opportunity to sit up close. Your average NBA team is not going to alienate a Season-Ticket Holder that spends big bucks for that privilege. Hornet personnel immediately whisked her from the bowels of the arena up to the Hornets Owner's Suite for the remainder of the game. Owner George Shinn while not condoning the action of Marion Bright was so amused that at a later date he personally presented Marion with her own solid Gold Peanut.

A game in front of nobody

Imagine a game that was played and no one was in the stands to enjoy it. That very thought became reality on January 3, 2002 in Charlotte, North Carolina. The Hornets were scheduled to host the Golden State Warriors. Charlotte was under the control of Paul Silas and the Warriors were piloted by Garry St Jean. It was to be an interesting night pitting each against the other. With the beer cold, popcorn hot and refreshment stands stocked the Hornets anticipated another decent crowd for a Tuesday night. But, Mother Nature would hear nothing of it. The Weather Service had issued a Winter Storm Advisory for the Central Piedmont Region of North Carolina putting Charlotte directly in its path. Add to the mix there was no local television scheduled only radio. So the only way to see the game was either in person or listen to the contest on the radio.

For the residents of the region it turned out to be a severe mixture of freezing rain, snow and ice. As is atypical of the south in winter was their in-ability to handle harsh winter weather. There were no snow plows, minimal road sanders and a traditional "we don't get much snow around here" attitude to warrant the expenditure for snow removal equipment. They figured in time it would all melt away with rising temperatures. By game time on the 3nd the weather conditions had drastically deteriorated. Under this weather advisory people were expected to navigate the roads and get to the Coliseum for the game. Driving in Charlotte that night was treacherous.

The NBA will play under various conditions cancelling games only when there was a serious issue of public safety. While driving conditions were poor, it was judged that fans could make it to the Coliseum and it was decided that the game would be played. Both teams were at the arena and the three men officiating crew was in place so the tip would happen at its normal time of 7:10pm. The Charlotte Coliseum sat high on a hill in southwest Charlotte a stone's throw from the Charlotte-Douglas Airport. Opened in 1988, the venue was built primarily to house the ACC and its tournaments every spring. It was spartanly built and was lacking in the suites and luxury perks and amenities that the NBA desired in its buildings'. When George Shinn was granted a franchise the 24,000 Coliseum was deemed more than adequate for the expansion franchise. And, the Coliseum was filled regularly to capacity of 24,042 for 364 straight home games. The sell-out streak started for the Hornets on December 23, 1988 when Kurt Rambis tipped in the game winner against Chicago for a 103-101 win and ended almost nine years later on November 24, 1997 against the Detroit Pistons with a 90-85 win and 22,617 persons in attendance. With the history of attendance backing the Hornets up, there was an anticipation of a decent crowd showing up even with the bad weather conditions.

The officiating crew working the game consisted of Louis Grillo, Blane Reichelt and Kevin Fehr. With Grillo in place at his center circle position at 7:09pm he blew his whistle and called for the teams to line up at center court for the tip. It was 7:10pm and this game was going to start on time. With play under way most of the Hornets Staff were amazed at what they noticed. The Charlotte Coliseum was empty. There were fans scattered throughout the building. These hearty folks made the journey from wherever they lived to the Coliseum to see the Hornets battle the Warriors. We looked around and tried to count how many paying customers there were? Most of us stopped at around 200. We discovered there were more people working as ushers, concessions and security then fans. Another phenomenon was you could hear everything that was uttered by both benches. Even the chatter between players was distinguishable. Both teams learned quickly to keep it quiet after seven quick technical fouls were called by the officials who had heard the players disparaging remarks. Charlotte had been hit with four technicals and the Warriors earned three of their own. If this had been a normal crowd in attendance none of the babble from the bench would have been heard and most likely zero technicals would have been called. For 48:00 minutes it was as if the two teams were playing for themselves. The crowd had absolutely no influence on how the game was being played. Before an announced crowd of 2,000 people the Hornets went on to beat the Golden State Warriors 114-102.

Where were these 2,000 people?   They were at a game that no one had seen.

Public Relations

Public Relations is the delivery of your message in a positive manner. It is used when there is a crisis and when there is good news. Every man, woman and child are the recipients of some form of PR every day. When something goes terribly wrong like the Gulf Oil Spill that occurred in April of 2010 the PR experts began a campaign of damage control that continues to this day. British Petroleum (BP) and their public relations machine was faced with the monumental task of putting a positive spin on what turned out to be the oil industry's largest spill in history? Mile after mile of the Gulf's fragile coastline was tainted. Marshlands as well as, numerous marine and aquatic animals from Texas to Florida were irreparably harmed. Public Relations in sports are hugely different from what the folks at BP were faced with.

In professional sports, the primary goal of the Public Relations Department is to generate positive stories on its players and coaches. Additionally, they are a service organization that provides statistical information for their home town media as well as, the visiting media assigned to cover the team. The PR Departments for the most part provide efficient means for distributing information. Most PR Departments go out of their way to service their media especially the visiting media. It was a common practice for the Home PR Department to assemble media packages which are crammed full of information on their team as well as, statistical information, game notes and credentials. These packets were dropped off at the visiting team's hotel and most of the times were found under our room door when we checked in. Today the NBA has some of the best public relations people in sports. This efficiency has evolved over the years and frankly was not always the case.

I can remember when we were travelling commercially and on many occasions we would end up leaving on the first flight of the day usually between 5 and 6 am. Leaving this early tended to make it a very long day for all of us. The talent was lucky, they could check into the team's hotel catch a few hours of sleep, have something to eat and finish their game preparation. For us production types it meant going straight to the arena to set-up for that night's broadcast. Most of the cities we visited the Public Relation Departments understood our predicament and they were more than accommodating to our needs. Our media packets and credentials were always waiting for us at the television mobile unit parked outside the venue.

You noticed that I said most of the cities we visited were great to work with the exception of one-Milwaukee. It was a city that I dreaded visiting especially in the winter. It was cold, dreary and snowy and the television mobile units we worked in were always outside in the elements. Putting the weather aside the main reason for my dislike of Milwaukee was not the city, its people or its building The Bradley Center. The Milwaukee Bucks had the worse Public Relations Director of all 30 NBA teams. There are not enough adjectives to describe this person. He went out of his way to make our job difficult.

One incident that sticks in my mind happened to me on a typical Milwaukee winter's day. My colleagues and I arrived mid-morning on a flight from Boston. The conditions at Milwaukee's Mitchell Field were horrible. We landed in a swirling snow storm and grabbed our bags for the treacherous trip into the city by taxicab. The talent Gil Santos and Bob Cousy were headed to our hotel and I headed to the arena. Arriving at the Bradley Center the first thing I noticed was there was no media packet waiting for me at the mobile unit.   The Bucks offices were located in the Bradley Center so I walked in and asked if I could please get some game notes and my credential.

They curtly responded "Your Packet is at your hotel!"

I responded back, "So you're telling me that if I want my stuff I have to pick it up at the hotel?"

Their answer was "Yep!"

I stormed out of the office, threw on my coat and proceeded to trudge through a Milwaukee snow storm for four blocks to the Hyatt Regency where I would be staying and I picked up my packet and slipped and slid back to the arena.

Later I'm in the truck working when I get a call from my promotion people back in Boston. They needed to make some copy changes and were wondering if I could take care of it so it would make air in the game. No problem! All I needed was a typewriter and some paper and I'd be all set. Remember, this was before there were lap tops, email and cell phones.

Well back inside the Bradley Center and once again I asked if I could please use a typewriter and some paper to make some changes?

Ever the cooperative people they looked at me and said "there will be a typewriter available in the Press Room after it opens at 5 o'clock." I looked at my watch it was 2pm and I needed to get my copy updated. You guessed it, back to the hotel through the snow into the Business Center to do what I had to do and back to the arena cold, wet and pissed off with ruined shoes to boot.

I was so upset I placed a call to the League's Public Relations Office and I filed a formal complaint complete with all the details on how my day went. As a footnote, their PR Director is gone and frankly the

Milwaukee Bucks are a much better organization without him. After all these years all I can do is laugh at what transpired.

Howie, Jeff, Harvey and Harold

In sharp contrast to the PR circus that was Milwaukee I will let you know that there are Public Relations people all over the league that provide the media with prompt, courteous and accurate information with pure professionalism. Having been associated with three different organizations there were four individuals all unique in the own way. My first introduction to PR at the NBA level was in Boston and their legend Howie McHugh. McHugh was with the Celtics from the beginning in 1946 until his passing in 1983. McHugh lived and breathed the Boston Celtics and was a storage vault of information on the fabled franchise. I learned quickly that Howie could be relied upon to get you any requested information in a timely manner. Toward the end of his career McHugh slowed down quite a bit. At the same time, late in Howie's tenure the NBA was just starting to grow; especially in the broadcast area. There was no NBA Entertainment division which today provides all the teams with video and audio support. For Howie and the rest of the league it was film; 16mm film and usually black & white. Highlights existed but they were just as hard to find. Howie, after numerous requests for footage finally came up with the perfect excuse for not being able to locate what you asked for.

When asked, he would simply respond, "Sorry kid, we lost it in the fire." Then he'd move on to another pressing PR issue. You would end up standing there nodding okay yet, in your mind you're thinking, "What fire?" In tribute and respect Larry Bird for his entire playing career kept a picture of Howie McHugh and a four-leaf clover above his locker for all to see. The Celtics have had only two Public Relations Directors in their sixty-eight year history.

Jeff Twiss, Howie's able replacement has been at the helm for the last thirty-one years. In Jeff's reign he has witnessed both the highs and the lows. He was the source for information when the team won championships and sadly when they were confronted with tragedy; Jeff was the face of the organization. His attitude and professionalism was present in all his dealings with the media. He never left you hanging for information. Requests for interviews and phone calls were returned promptly. He has quietly done his job for all these years. I can still say after being away from the Celtics for over 24 years I still get my calls returned and my questions answered.

Harvey Pollack was and is in addition to being the PR Director of the 76ers; Harvey is the "Stat King" of the NBA. Harvey was around in the beginning working through the infancy of the NBA and is still at it at ninety-two. If there was an unusual statistic, Harvey would have it in his guide. Everyone associated with the NBA anticipated its publication and everybody in the league could not wait to get their copy of Harvey's statistical yearbook. Harvey had many firsts. Rebounds were never a separate entity. Now, thanks to Harvey we count offensive and defensive rebounds. No one cared about shots blocked now thanks to Pollack it is a regular statistic. Imagine sifting through every box score that was issued; Harvey did and it resulted in the most complete information source ever to be created for the NBA. Another side of Harvey was his ability to be frugal especially with his owner's money.

Most of the teams in the NBA catered reasonably wholesome meals in their Press Room for visiting and home media. This was not the case in Philadelphia. For years you were lucky if you received a soft-drink or cup of coffee. It improved briefly when Harvey and the Sixers added small, individual bags of potato chips. This lack of cuisine continued for quite a while. Moving forward to our annual league meetings where we're in an open session discussing PR issues when Harvey takes the floor. His complaint to the league and the group assembled; "everybody is using his telephones to make long-distance calls and it was costing him money." Heading the break-out session was NBA Public Relations Vice President, Brian McIntyre. Brian's quick and witty response put Harvey back in his seat. "Harvey, if you spent some of the money you saved from the scrumptious meal you served, I don't think there would be a problem."

Harold Kaufman was the Publicity Director for the Charlotte/ New Orleans Hornets for just under a quarter of a century. Harold spent most of his career doing his due diligence for Hornets Owner, George Shinn. George was a loyal, likeable guy who was a successful business man with entrepreneurial expertise that catapulted him into the Owners Club that was the NBA. Unfortunately faced with several misguided mistakes made outside the realm of basketball from owner issues to relocation Harold's job was that much more difficult. I give him credit it was difficult having to juggle his team and its owners through challenging times in Charlotte and New Orleans. Harold was not with the organization for two seasons while it was in Oklahoma City. He rejoined the team when it returned to New Orleans after Katrina. If I were to assess his legacy, it would be the large number of people that worked for him and the Hornets that moved on to positions with other teams in the NBA as well as with other teams in other sports. From all indications, they are all prospering.

Chapter 12

Venues

<u>New Orleans</u>

The New Orleans Arena now known as The Smoothie King Center was the scene of one of the Hornets and NBA's most embarrassing moments. All caught on-camera live for a national audience on TNT to witness. Hosting the San Antonio Spurs in the opening game of the Second Round of the 2008 Playoffs, the moment came at the end of the first quarter.

The New Orleans Hornets (now Pelicans) have a reputation as one of the elite teams when it comes to in-arena fan entertainment. Their dancers-The Honeybees are among the leading dance teams in the nation. Hugo the Hornet was a pioneer in mascot skits that are performed today by most other mascots on the other teams. On this particular evening Hugo was to perform a skit that he had done many times before; the jump through the hoop. Basically, the skit was performed by Hugo and a couple of his "Beekeeper" assistants. It was simple in its execution and provided a big reward especially when it was customized for the television audience. Hugo was to run up to a spring board, explode through a giant metal and paper hoop with the words "Welcome everyone watching on TNT." And, he would finish with a thunderous dunk to the delight of the crowd. The only difference this night was the hoop was to be lit on fire to increase the thrill factor of his jumping through the flaming hoop. Hugo and his crew executed the skit with perfection and the crowd went wild with cheers and applause. Only, there was a slight problem after the dunk.

The fire on the hoop could not be extinguished. It had to be put out with fire extinguishers. Now, the residue from the fire extinguishers on the court had to be cleaned up. The floor had become slippery and it could cause injury to the players. Both teams were on the sidelines waiting and waiting. Time stretched to an unheard of network television delay of well over 20 minutes as the cleanup crew continued removing the chemical residue left by the extinguishers. Finally with the playing surface satisfactory play was resumed.

Two things happened as a result of that night of May 3, 2008; the Hornets prevailed to take a 1-0 second round lead over the current World Champion San Antonio Spurs.

And, The Wheel of Fire was banned by the NBA never to be used in any arena by any team ever again.

Boston

Nothing will ever equal the excitement that was the 1986 NBA Playoffs. If you were lucky enough to be inside the Boston Garden or watching on television this one Conference Semi-Final game against the Atlanta Hawks you were treated to a true basketball spectacle.

First, let's meet the players: John Salley, the future first round pick for the Detroit Pistons. Then there was Brent Musburger, CBS Play-By-Play Announcer with his partner former coach and player Billy Cuningham and Susan Sykes aka Busty Heart. It was the night Busty Heart met John Salley and Brent Musburger went speechless as the Boston Celtics unintentionally introduced their newest secret weapon.

Mid-way through the Third Quarter with the Celtics holding a slim 54-48 lead over Atlanta Musburger delivered an obligatory promotion and segued into a discussion of the upcoming NBA Draft. As he started talking about potential draft picks the director cut to a shot of a young man that Brent quickly identified as John Salley a potential first-round pick. All of a sudden, the proverbial "crap hit the fan." Sitting next to John was a rather well-endowed young lady who noticing she was "on-camera" began to jiggle her ample breasts for all to see on national Television. Salley sitting there was not sure what **to** do. Immediately the director cut away from her and right back to game action but it was too late. Brent was flustered and Susan Sykes aka Busty Heart and her size 46D breasts had made her television debut leaving Brent Musburger speechless.

His Partner Billy Cunnigham egged him on with "What did you say Brent" Then they both lost it into laughter as they worked on getting their composure back.

In the 1980's there were few mascots, halftime shows and fewer dance teams. In Boston the running joke was when Director of Public Relations Jeff Twiss put out his team's game notes under Halftime Entertainment he would write, "Ball Boy puts ball rack at center court." This was a reference to Boston's tradition of winning basketball over entertainment. Quite a bit has changed since then. Boston has a mascot and yes, a dance team. It would be safe to say that Red Auerbach is shaking his head somewhere knowing his beloved Celtics had abandoned some of their old traditions in favor of a modern approach to entertain the fans in attendance.

With Busty's appearance in 1986 for a brief moment the fans of Boston had a new un-official mascot even if you could only see her in person. The networks were not going to make the same mistake twice.

Fireworks

As mentioned, the Hornets were noted for their big-bang pyro player introductions before the tip-off of every game. There is also a running joke around the league that when a player is "hot," the only way to stop him is by his own coach. On this particular night in New Orleans it would not be the coach that stopped a streaking player. It would be a pyrotechnic explosion that became the villain.

Jamal Mashburn, a New Yorker by birth attended the University of Kentucky and was drafted in the First Round by the Dallas Mavericks in 1993. Known for his deadly accurate shooting, Mashburn hung around the NBA for twelve seasons. With stops in Miami and Charlotte/New Orleans Mashburn earned the reputation as a scorer that you could depend on while reaching all-star status. Acquired in a trade to Charlotte from Miami in 2000, Mashburn joined a Hornets team weak on experience but high on energy.

On the night of January 15, 2003 the Hornets were hosting the Los Angeles Lakers and it was to be a night when not a coach or injury stopped a player from playing. It would be the venue in New Orleans. Riding a 155 game starting streak Mashburn was getting ready to be introduced with his fellow starters: Baron Davis, David Wesley, P J Brown and Jamal Magloire.

With the house lights out the video screens glaring and the introduction audio screaming the ritual of announcing the starters had begun. Public Address Announcer Jim Rumsfeld growled out his usual, "Ladies and gentlemen, get on your feet and welcome tonight's starters for your New Orleans Hornets. Starting at forward number 42- P J Brown..." and as each player came running out of the tunnel to a crescendo of pyro explosions timed to go off after each player's name as they ran out on the court. Timing was the key. As Mashburn ran out onto the court the explosion went off and kicked up the usual residue after an explosive discharge. Mashburn met the explosive dust and found some of it had lodged in his eyes.

The house lights came up full, the referees signaled for the teams to line up for the opening tip and they were ready for the game to begin. Only problem there was five Lakers and only four Hornets at the center circle. Over at the Hornets bench, Head Trainer Terry Kofler was busy rinsing Mashburn's eyes of the ash and cinder that was irritating him. The officials would have none of that and immediately ordered the Hornets to get a fifth player on the court so the game could begin. Hornets Head Coach Tim Floyd sent George Lynch in for Mashburn and the game started with Mashburn missing start number 156.

Mashburn eventually went on to play 45 minutes scoring 19 points in a game that the Hornets lost by a score of 90-82. The official reason given for Mashburn not being able to start; he had a contact lens problem. We now know differently!

Bath Time

When was the last time you went to an NBA game and instead of basketball being played you took a bath? On November 4, 1995 the San Antonio Spurs opened their season hosting the Golden State Warriors. The Spurs were in their third season playing in the newly constructed Alamo Dome. Opening night is a big deal all around the league as each team goes the extra effort to create a knock-down, intense multi-faceted player introduction that is a video and audio sensory treat. This night in the Alamo City it would be no different. Patrons were presented with a thunderous high-powered pyrotechnic display that had the Alamo Dome rocking.

There was only one slight problem. Someone had forgotten to disarm the triggers of the dome's fire-fighting equipment.   As the dome filled with noise and smoke from the staged explosions, the high-powered water cannons that were spaced around the upper deck of the Alamo Dome sensed the smoke and promptly kicked on spewing the assembled sell-out crowd with an estimated 15,000 gallons of water. Players seeing what happening ran as fast as they could toward the locker rooms to get out from under the deluge as water began to soak the floor and the opening night attendees. Finally the rush of water subsided. In its wake were thousands of water soaked fans who bore the brunt from the man-made deluge. Spectators then had to sit through a 50 minute indoor rain delay and cleanup before the game could even start.

Not an International Incident

I had the honor and prestige of traveling with the Celtics to Madrid, Spain for the McDonalds Open in 1988. The Celtics would meet Spain's number one team Real Madrid and the second game of the trip would be against the Yugoslavian National Team. This would be the first time that a team from the NBA would have an opportunity to meet some of Europe's best players. This tournament happened just three years before the conflict that would break up Yugoslavia. It would take ten years of harsh fighting between Orthodox Christian Serbians, Catholic Croatians and Muslim Bosnians to end and only then after a forceful intervention by the international community. Finally, the "last great war in Europe" came to an end in 2006.

The Celtics faced some fierce competition from the Yugoslavs. Their roster was a who's who of future NBA players. Vlade Divac, Drazen Petrovic, Toni Kukoc and Dino Radja led this multi-talented team of Serbs, Bosnians and Croats against the Celtics. The Yugoslavs were united in Madrid when they played Boston. It wasn't until one unforgiving incident later in the 1988 FIBA Championships. Vlade Divac a Serbian took offense and pushed away a fan who stormed on the court waving a flag from Croatia. The flag incident splintered personal relationships and ended lifelong friendships as the Yugoslavian team members took sides in the dispute.

If you want to learn more about this conflict that turned friends into enemies, I urge you to watch the ESPN "30 for 30" Documentary *"Once Brothers"* my friend Dino Cocoros from NBA Entertainment produced this wonderfully accurate film on the breakup of friends because of religion, political bickering and strife.

Meanwhile returning to our trip to Spain our entourage included: me and my announcers Bob Cousy and Mike Crispino. I was assisted by my WLVI-TV Production Manager Gail Satz along with Producer Bill Fairweather and Photographer Jimmy Clark and we were scheduled to join up with Turner Broadcasting in Madrid and produce and direct a joint feed back to the States. We traveled British Airways Business Class on the overnight flight from Boston to London and then on to Madrid. Arriving at the Adolfo Suarez Airport in Madrid our photo support crew jumped off the plane to document our arrival. Big mistake! Before we knew it, we were surrounded by machine gun touting Para militaries screaming at us in Spanish with their guns loaded and leveled. We were quickly rounded up and taken to a secure area inside the airport where we were questioned about what had happened. Finally, we were informed that it was against Spanish Law to photograph both inside and outside the terminal. There was only one thing I could do. I asked for the video tape cassette and I stomped on it and gave the now useless video cassette to the security official and we were let go to continue our trip covering the Celtics in Madrid.

Oklahoma City

August 29, 2005 remains vivid in my mind. It was early in the morning when the winds and water of Hurricane Katrina smashed into the Gulf Coast of Louisiana and Mississippi. It was hard to imagine what had happened to my New Orleans. With over 80% of the city underwater its people struggled to survive to the point of near anarchy. For folks that stayed and rode it out, their very existence was tested beyond belief. For those of us who were fortunate to have the means to evacuate; we witnessed the devastation from afar and it was heartbreaking to watch.

The Hornets were informed that New Orleans and the surrounding areas were so overwhelmed by the storm a decision was made by all parties concerned that the team had to find a temporary home until such time New Orleans was recovered and ready to take them back. In two short weeks, the conclusion was made to temporarily move the franchise to Oklahoma City. My wife Sharyn and I had a fortnight to pack our belongings and secure our home in Slidell, Louisiana before moving 954 miles to Oklahoma. Another Hornets family living in Slidell was our Equipment Manager David Jovanovic and his wife Mary-Ellen and daughters Gracie and Abby. Their house had sustained major damage from the storm and was uninhabitable. Our House survived the storm and became their home until their house was repaired and ready for them to move back in. David would be going to Oklahoma alone and my wife would be accompanying me. We all headed for Oklahoma City not knowing what to expect.

Our new, temporary home was the Ford Center. Built at a reasonable cost of 92 million to the city, it was Spartan in its amenities and facilities. Oklahomans have a saying and its "Get 'er done! And, they did just that. In a period of just under a month's time Oklahoma

City transformed the Ford Center into an 18,000 seat arena to host the displaced Hornets. There were many obstacles and challenges for all team departments when we arrived. From a broadcasting point of view, the building was not ready to handle television. At best it was barely able to support one mobile unit. Crewing was another concern. Finding a permanent crew base was difficult. There were not enough qualified freelancers to support one broadcast let alone a second or third broadcast crew. We settled in for a long season. Eventually all that was needed came to fruition. Our infrastructure at the Ford Center was brought up to specifications. The small crew base surprised me with their technical savvy and willingness to adapt to the demands of games on an ongoing basis. Everything we worried about upon or arrival to Oklahoma disappeared. We were humming right along.

Living in Oklahoma turned out to be a great experience. We were treated royally. We were welcomed with open arms. Oklahoma City and its surrounding area had something to prove. It wanted to show the world that it was a big league city and the fan base accepted us with enthusiasm. They truly loved their sports in Oklahoma. On one Saturday November 12, 2005, Oklahoma City proved it was ready for the big time. It started at noon when the University of Oklahoma hosted the "Aggies" of Texas A & M University in front of 82,000 people in Norman, Oklahoma. The "Sooners" were followed by the "Cowpokes" of Oklahoma State with a game in Stillwater against Texas Tech in front of an estimated crowd of 60,000 plus. The Coup d'état was later that very Saturday evening when the Hornets hosted the Dallas Mavericks in front of a sellout crowd of over 18,000 fans at The Ford Center. Oklahoma fans came out in droves to attend these events.

For two seasons the Hornets called Oklahoma City home. The people were fervent in their support of the team. We spent two memorable years there. Some fans became lifelong friends. We were

grateful to folks like Bill Hurley and Emma Hurley of Clearchannel
Radio who helped ease the pain of relocating to a new city. Terry
Wiens and his wife Jo welcomed us to their city and into their home. At
every home game you'd see Terry resplendent as ever in a full length
"Beekeeper's" suit cheering for his adopted team. When was the last
time you had a friend name a new born horse after you? Well, Terry
and Jo did; "Lewie" the little foal was last seen happily running and
grazing at the Wiens Ranch in Edmond, Oklahoma. We left Oklahoma
City knowing that one day the city would eventually be able to support
an NBA team. That day came in 2007 when the Seattle Supersonics was
purchased by a group of Oklahoma businessmen and the franchise was
moved to Oklahoma City and renamed the Thunder.

   A few endearing moments you might or might not know about
Oklahoma and Oklahoma City. I could not to get used to looking out
my twenty story office window in downtown Oklahoma City and
seeing cattle grazing and jack pumps working to pump the "black gold"
out of the ground. Everywhere we went we would see these jack
pumps working. At the airport, downtown and even in people's back
yards the oil business was big business. We never got used to hearing
tornado warnings blaring and alerting us to take cover. Driving on the
interstate was a treat. In most states you drive through counties. In
Louisiana you motor through parishes. In Oklahoma you drive
through both counties and reservations-Indian reservations. Hands
down the best civic pride presentation ever, occurred every Friday
afternoon at 5pm, when radio station KOMA 92.5FM would sound a
factory whistle and segue into Rodgers and Hammerstein's
"Oklahoma" for its regular listeners.

Epilogue

So, how does one person weigh their career and its legacy? It is simple! In my case I have been fortunate to have participated in a field of endeavor that began when I was thirteen years old and still continues after six decades of doing a job that I love.

I was there when television was in black and white and in standard definition. I participated in the transition to color television and now I am amazed at the technology that has continued to grow and presented us with high definition television and 3-D viewing in our homes. I was part of the transition of an industry that moved from cameras with racking lens and "push-rod" zooms to hand held high definition cameras that are phenomenal. In the middle 1960's video tape was two inches wide and bulky. Video tape machines that recorded programming were large and heavy. Now, we are in a tapeless world where all recording is handled digitally. I grew up in the age of the vacuum tube and was wowed when the transistor was introduced. Now broadcast technology is based on computers, semi-conductors and chips. We're in the digital age and the state of technology has changed. There is one constant; we still cover the games the same way with the goal of providing the viewer with coverage that makes them feel like they're cheering in the arena while sitting comfortably at home.

What is my legacy? Wow! At first I had to think of what it would be? Then it hit me, it's the people. Mentors like Dick Lipson, Joe Quasarano, Powell Kidd and Jim Moriarty provided sound input and support. All over the country I see the managers, announcers, technicians, coaches, referees and players that started when I did and now they have all matured just like me.

Sports heroes like Bill Russell and Bob Cousy are now 80 and 85 years old. Sadly, we're losing that first generation that I and my friends worshiped as young men and teenagers. Now, the sons of players who I knew are now active ball players. Stephen Curry and his brother Seth are examples. I remember them stopping by regularly to play ball at the training facility in Charlotte while waiting for their father Dell Curry to finish up practice.

The names continue: Tim Hardaway Jr., Glenn Rice Jr., Austin Daye, Mike Dunleavy Jr., Luke Walton, Gerald Henderson Jr. and Austin Rivers all are sons of players that I covered professionally.

When I'm asked to speak at a college or university on the subject of sports broadcasting and its opportunities, I am quite honest with the aspiring talent, producers, directors and technicians. I tell these future broadcast "want-to-be's" to stick with their dreams and be persistent in their pursuit of what they want to obtain. They ask me how they can get started. My answer surprises most of the students. In my humble opinion the problem that most of the current crop of future broadcasters is they lack two very important items on their resumes. What is missing for these individuals is they lack a strong sense of history and as well as, their ability to write with and use colorful language. So, my advice is to continue with your creative writing classes and make an effort to study and understand history and it place in society.

It seems that everyone wants to be a star and no one wants to explore the opportunities that exist behind the camera. There is an entire generation of broadcasters about to retire and there are jobs and money to be made in both the talent and technical sides of broadcasting.

The question we are all asking is where will the next generation of technical directors, audio, camera, video tape and graphics operators be coming from? If I were to offer additional guidance I would recommend a thorough knowledge of computer science. The broadcast industry is changing and almost all equipment is becoming computer software based. Yes, we still need people to man the equipment; but we also need the people with computer savvy and skills to operate the newest tapeless replay machines as well as, the sophisticated graphic machines.

Where would you start if you are interested in reporting or anchoring?

First, do not think you're going to land that first job in a top market. Get that out of your head immediately. The only position that may exist is a paid internship that exposes you to the "glitzy" side of broadcasting. Big deal if you're a page at one of the networks in New York or Los Angeles it will not give you the experience you will need to secure a paid position later in broadcasting. You are going to have to pay your dues and work your way up the ladder. In fact, you will be better off working in a smaller market where you will have the opportunity to learn. In small-town America you will be a "One-Man Band." You will be required to do everything at the station. Here is where the true learning process will begin.

Once assigned a story, you will hit the field running. You will set-up your own camera. Next you will shoot your interviews as well as your identifying stand-up followed by a trip back to the newsroom where you will then write your story and go into the edit bay and finish editing, voice tracking and timing your story. Upon completion you pass off the edited story for playback and you head out to the anchor desk where suddenly you are live after being introduced by the host. If it sounds like a tremendous amount of work well folks, it is. Yes, it is hard work but it gives the individual an understanding of what it takes to get the job done. This small market exposure will be your stepping stone to bigger and better markets. As your experience level grows so will your confidence.

For the folks that are interested in the technical side, I suggest a similar career path. In smaller markets you will have the opportunity to learn everything. Big market restrictions can hinder your career rather than help. In larger markets television and radio stations are more specialized and may require union participation. This is not a barrier it's just an obstacle that may limit what you can do and cannot do as well as, dictate what you can operate and not operate. It is ardently suggested you have your skill level in place before you attempt the rat race of major market television that is New York, Los Angeles or Chicago. Trust me; you will learn more in a smaller market then in a top twenty market.

Be hungry! Check your ego at the door! Remember you are entering the workforce like everyone else. Just because you have a four-year communications degree from an elite communications school; it doesn't mean squat! All it proved was your ability to stick to something for four years without losing interest. Keep your resume short and to-the-point. Make sure you are specific to the job you are interested in. Do not take a mass mailing or a group emailing approach. We can tell when a cover letter is nothing more than a cut and paste job. Chances are this type of inquiry usually ends up in the delete file. I want someone who has taken the time to research the position they are interested in as well as, the person who will be doing the hiring. Your cover letter should be concise and just one page. Frankly, I do not care if you worked six months at the mall selling retail. I want to know what practical experience you have gained and what courses you have taken to make you an attractive candidate. Ask yourself the question, does he care that I sold shoes part time or would he like to know that I've spent time around the university's radio station learning to edit using current industry software? I want to see something that jumps up and grabs my attention. Stop and think about the number of students that upon graduation flood broadcasting stations all over the country. They are your competition. We are inundated with hundreds of applicants every spring who are desperate to break-in to the industry.

Broadcasting can be a humbling experience and at the same time a very rewarding career. You will have to hold your emotions close when you're reporting on a tragedy and be constantly objective. Do not pre-judge! Appreciate what you have and work hard to maintain it. Do not be stubborn, Adapt or die!

Good Luck! I hope someday to meet you as my replacement.

Made in the USA
Charleston, SC
27 February 2015